THE BORDERS

F. R. Banks

THE BORDERS

B. T. Batsford Ltd

London

First published 1977

Copyright F. R. Banks 1977
Printed in Great Britain by
J. W. Arrowsmith Ltd., Bristol

for the Publishers B. T. Batsford Ltd
4 Fitzhardinge Street, London W1H 0AH

ISBN 0 7134 0289 X

Contents

Acknowledgments

The Author and Publishers would like to thank the following for their permission to reproduce their photographs in this book:

John Beecham, no. 21; Leonard & Marjorie Gayton, no. 6; the Noel Habgood collection, no. 16; A. F. Kersting, nos 2, 3, 5, 7, 8, 11, 14, 15, 17, 18, 19, 20, 21, 23, 25, 26; John Topham/Kenneth Scowen, nos 4, 12, 22; Derek Widdicombe, nos 9, 10, 13, 24.

Thanks are also due to Messrs Longmans, Green & Co. for kind permission to quote from G. M. Trevelyan's essay, 'The Middle Marches', published in the volume, *Clio, a Muse.*

The map is by David R. Banks

Illustrations

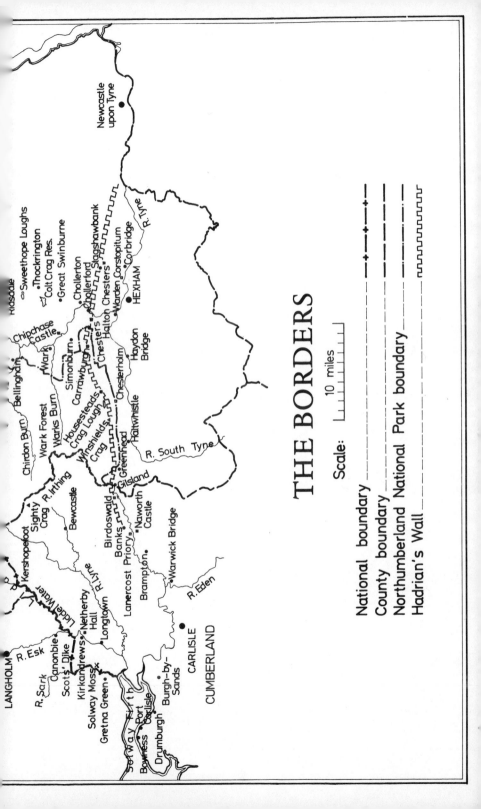

THE BORDERS

Scale: 10 miles

National boundary
County boundary
Northumberland National Park boundary
Hadrian's Wall

CHAPTER ONE

The Border Country

The Border Country — what romance the name conjures up, what visions of raid and counter-raid by Scots and English, of skirmish and family feud, of rival factions clashing, of moss-troopers riding over hill and through dale, of the constant watching for the raider by ford and pass, the hard but vigorous life of 'spur, spear and snaffle' sung in many a Border ballad. From the coming of the Romans in the 1st century, through the struggles of the early Christians, the invasion of the Normans, and the long-drawn-out conflict between England and Scotland until the Union of the Crowns in 1603, the Border was the scene of perpetual strife.

During medieval times much of life near the Border was taken up with predatory raids from one side or the other, rewarded, if fortune favoured, with cattle 'reived' from the enemy's farmsteads. Though these raids persisted for little more than 400 years (from the late twelfth century to the beginning of the seventeenth), constant resistance to a common enemy, not only from across the Border, but often from the neighbouring valleys as well, served to cement the affairs as well the relationships of each family and made an impression on the Borderer which was not effaced for centuries.

In addition to these purely local squabbles, the Border was too often the battleground over which was fought out the bitter struggle between the rival kingdoms of England and Scotland. The conquest of most of England by the Normans in 1066 threw the Northern counties and the neighbouring parts of Scotland into a state of anarchy which continued until the defeat and death of Malcolm Canmore of Scotland in 1093 at the Battle of Alnwick; and in the twelfth century David I gained a hold over Northumberland that was assisted by the disturbances during the feeble reign of Stephen. Later in the century William the Lion invaded England, and he was forced to make peace only after his capture at Alnwick. Cumberland, too, did not escape its share of trouble; it became part of the British kingdom of Strathclyde in 945 and was finally annexed to England only in 1157.

The repeated efforts of Edward I (that 'hammer of the Scots') and his son, Edward II, to subjugate Scotland, and the retaliation of John Baliol, Edward's nominee to the Scottish crown, of the patriotic Wallace and the redoubtable Bruce, kept the Border in a state of ferment from the end of the thirteenth century on. Trouble began again towards the end of the fourteenth century, with the Earl of Douglas leading a foray into England which took him as far as Durham. Throughout the following two centuries, the period of the Stewarts, the whole of Scotland was in a state of turmoil, and this disquiet was nowhere more strongly felt than in the Border. James IV and James V both invaded England and harried Northumberland, in support first of the insurrection of Perkin Warbeck, then of the French, on whom England had declared war. Both eventually met with crippling defeats, and in revenge Henry VIII ordered a counter-invasion, in 1544. Though his forces were scattered on Ancrum Moor in the following year his general, the ruthless Earl of Hertford, laid waste the Scottish side of the Border, razing farms and villages, and destroying the splendid abbeys of Kelso and Jedburgh, Melrose and Dryburgh. Peace came at last with the Union of the Crowns in the person of James VI and I, but it was many years before the Border settled down to a less acrimonious and more profitable form of life.

One cannot travel far in the Border Country without experiencing that subtle and pervasive atmosphere with which it has been imbued by long centuries of conflict. 'Here is abundant business for the antiquary', wrote Daniel Defoe in the early seventeenth century, in the course of his tour through England and Scotland, 'every place shows you ruin'd castles, Roman altars, inscriptions, monuments of battles, of heroes killed, . . .' Evidence of conflict survives in the remains of closely-guarded castle and pillaged monastery, and even more in the numerous pele towers or tower-houses, those medieval fortified dwellings that are a characteristic feature of the Border.

The term *pele*, derived like pale and palisade from the Latin *palus*, a stake, originally meant a palisaded enclosure and it has been adopted only comparatively recently to describe a defence work of this kind. A pele usually consists of a singular rectangular tower, of two or three storeys, with a vaulted basement into which cattle could be driven (or where goods could be stored) and living apartments for the family above; the connecting staircase is often arranged in a corner projection. It had a steeply-pitched roof, the walls being carried above this to form a crenellated parapet, and of necessity very small windows. Upwards of a hundred of these towers are yet to be seen in the Border counties, though some were places of occasional refuge only and not intended as permanent dwellings. Many of them were built during the fourteenth century, but restored and often enlarged in the sixteenth century.

These grim memorials from an unsettled past now serve to accentuate the essentially peaceful scenery of green, rounded upland (eminently suitable for its staple function of sheep rearing) and rich tree-embowered dale, supporting a mainly agricultural community. The type of farming carried on is dependent to a large extent on the underlying geological structure, and much of the Border Country is made up of various kinds of sedimentary rocks revealed in the form of sandstones, especially the grey-brown fell-sandstones, seen at their best in the escarpments of the Simonside Hills and similar ranges, on the Northumberland side, and the rich-hued red sandstones characteristic of Cumberland and the Scottish side of the Border.

The most dramatic scenic feature in the Border is the result of a volcanic intrusion of dark basaltic rock. This carries Hadrian's Wall for the most interesting part of its course; it strikes diagonally across Northumberland to reach the sea in the cliffs of Bamburgh and Dunstanburgh, and it extends out to Holy Island and the pinnacles of the Farne Islands. The basalt, varying from about 20 to 100 feet in thickness, lies almost horizontally between strata of the sedimentary rocks, but because of its greater hardness it has persisted where these have weathered away, and it now shows as a high, sharp-faced escarpment, broken off here and there into great upstanding crags.

In human terms, the Border is a land of scattered farmsteads. The villages are relatively few and widely spaced; they are mostly small and the houses are usually huddled together, conveying an impression of watchful defence. The towns in the Border, too (except for Carlisle), are invariably small and compact. Such industries as have grown up in them are for the most part both unobtrusive and indigenous to the soil, and the townsfolk, unlike those of overgrown cities, have remained in close contact with the countryside. The proximity of an ever-alert enemy instilled in those on both sides of the Border a self-reliance and rough courage, and this spirit has persisted as a strong feature of the Borderer's character.

A great deal of controversy has been created by attempts to prove that the present Border line is drawn arbitrarily and that other alternatives would have been quite as adequate. This, however, is far from being so. Although it may appear, from glancing at a map, that the boundary line might have taken some other course, one has only to explore along the Border and to learn about the people on either side to be convinced that, apart perhaps from a short length at the extreme west end, the Border could not easily have been fixed in any other position.

At the eastern end the broad, swift Tweed, so liable to flood, forms an obvious boundary. Between the river and the Cheviot Hills, which carry the Border over a major part of its course, lies a short stretch of undulating but not difficult country. The country on either side of the frontier in this section remained a kind of no-man's land, but thereafter the Border runs for many miles along a succession of high ridges presenting an almost continuous barrier. The Kershope Burn and the Liddel Water, which the boundary follows towards the west, are much more easily bridged or forded than the Tweed, a fact illustrated by this being in the Middle Ages the most savage part of the Border and the territory on either side the most often violated. Yet these waters do provide a natural boundary, and their valleys are skirted by open moorlands that would have been less easy to defend.

The short stretch of mainly level terrain between the Liddel Water and the River Esk on the one hand to the River Sark on the other, and extending to the alluvial regions of the Solway Firth, seems to me to prove the case for the present Border line by its exception. Long known as the Debatable Land, it was 'no other thing but theft, reiff, and slaughter' until a boundary was finally agreed on by the two nations in 1552. An earthwork, known as the Scots' Dike, was constructed from the Esk, starting from a point just below the junction of the Liddel, across to the Sark, which the boundary then followed to its mouth in the Solway.

Some persons, good Northumbrians among them, have argued that the natural boundary between England and Scotland is the Tyne Gap. A boundary here would transfer most of Northumberland as well as part of Cumberland to Scotland, and the argument for it is usually based on three factors: the line along the valley of the South Tyne and its western extension, the Irthing, is shorter than the existing Border line; the scenery of Northumberland (the north and west regions, at least) resembles that of southern Scotland rather than that of County Durham (which is no doubt true); and the Northumbrian himself is more closely akin to the Scottish Lowlander than the native of Durham. But boundaries of countries depend not on landscape and kinship, but on defensible frontiers, and the Tyne, even as far downstream as Corbridge, is normally much too easily forded to have provided an effective barrier. And the Northumbrian himself, though he may differ in many ways from the man of Durham, has still less in common with the Scotsman. Not only in speech, but in temperament, in bearing, in underlying character, the Northumbrian has more sympathy with other people of the North of England than with the Scot.

But the Romans, it may be argued, chose to draw their boundary from the Tyne to the Solway. They certainly did, but then they required an elaborate system of military works to maintain it. Only the great Wall of Hadrian and its supporting defences prevented the wild Picts from intermingling, if not actually joining forces with, the scarcely less wild Brigantes of what is now northern England. The Romans, in effect, established that there should be a boundary, and thereby created a division that lasted for nearly 1,600 years, but with the collapse of the Roman administration and the readjustment of forces in this region, the Border came to assume a more natural and more easily defended line.

The transition did not take place at once. After the last of the Roman military forces had left, early in the 5th century, the Border Country, like the rest of Britain, was in a state of flux. The kingdom of Bernicia, established by new invaders, the Angles, extended at its greatest limit from the Tees to the Forth, but it had no recognised boundaries. The earliest section of the Border line to be established, that following the Tweed, was not acknowledged until after the Battle of Carham in 1018, and the rest did not begin to assume its present course until after the Norman Conquest, in about 1092, when William Rufus began the castle at Carlisle and planted foreign settlers in the town. The boundary from the

Tweed to the Esk was finally agreed on, after several abortive attempts at a solution, in 1244.

Attempts to frame laws to govern the relations between England and Scotland and to restrain the growing lawlessness of the Border were made at this time. Representatives of the two nations laid down that no-one of either country, even though he possessed land in the other, could be impeached anywhere but at the Border March, i.e. on the actual frontier. This right had been in existence as a principle for some time; Malcolm Canmore had claimed it in 1093 when William Rufus proposed transferring a Border dispute to the jurisdiction of his own council. Later, the frontier regions became organised into three defence zones, known as the East, Middle and West Marches, and the English side was governed (in theory at least) by a body known augustly as the Council of the North.

Other rights of Border law were determined in 1249, when those living within the bounds of the East March were required to report at the Redden (or Riding) Burn, where the Border line leaves the Tweed, and those of the Middle March at Gammel's Path near the head of the River Coquet, while those of the West March were to answer at Lamyford, near Kershopehead, where Northumberland, Cumberland and Scotland meet. It was agreed that a bondman who had sought refuge across the Border could be recovered by his master or his master's bailiff within 40 days, but after that period had elapsed his master had to secure a writ from the sovereign of the country to which the refugee had escaped before he could seize the offender. Stolen goods had similarly to be sued for by a writ in the court of the master on whose land they were found, but if the possessor then claimed them, the question had to be settled by a duel or combat, to take place on the March itself. This became a fundamental principle of Border law. Proof by witnesses was not regarded as evidence and trial by jury was not acknowledged; the matter could be decided only by a personal contest between the disputants. Any man could be called to the Marches for the purpose of combat 'except only the persons of the Kings of the said realms and the Bishops of St Andrews and Durham'. In a dispute concerning horses, cattle or pigs, combat could be evaded by the receiver, provided that he first recognised the accuser's claim as being just, then drove back the animals in question 'to the mid-stream of Tweed or Esk'.

Lords Wardens of the Marches were appointed, to administer justice along the Border, during the stormy reign of Edward I, and thereafter a definite set of laws slowly became established, though based on former customs. By the law of the 'hot trod', often referred to in Border tale and ballad, the aggrieved person, with his followers, was permitted to cross the Border 'without let or hindrance' up to six days after the stealing of any cattle and recover his property (if he could lay hands on it), provided that certain conditions were conformed to. For example, he was obliged to follow his lawful 'trod' or mission 'with hue and cry, with hound and horn', and he must carry a burning peat on the tip of his lance to make clear the mission he was on. A law-breaker escaping across the Border could seek sanctuary by ringing the bells at the first church he came to, and he could not then be seized and brought back.

Another law of the Marches very strictly observed was that no two persons living on opposite sides of the Border could intermarry without the agreement of both their Wardens. This agreement was in practice very difficult to obtain; the penalty for breaking the law was nothing less than death, and a like penalty was imposed on any priest who married such a couple without obtaining a licence beforehand from both Wardens.

Towards the end of the Middle Ages, as a result of the incessant bickerings between the two nations, moral corruption had become quite common, and many Borderers who had started as honest patriots deteriorated into nothing more than petty thieves. New laws became necessary to deal with these malefactors, and the *leges marchiarum* were extended in the effort to bring these hardy and reckless rebels to order. An international court was created under an assurance of trust, carried out at meetings of the Wardens of the corresponding English and Scottish Marches. A place and time were decided between the Wardens concerned and promulgated in the market towns on each side of the Border. Anyone who felt himself aggrieved by a person of the rival nation could then lodge a complaint with the clerk of his own Warden, who in turn informed the corresponding clerk across the Border. On the day agreed the Wardens arrived at the appointed place, each with his own retinue (often a necessary part of the proceedings, in view of the frequent disputes between the Wardens themselves, who were not always as impartial as the law expected them to be). After renewing their solemn assurance of trust, they nominated a jury of 12, the Scottish Warden selecting six Englishmen and the English Warden likewise six Scots. The jury then

considered the individual complaints and, upon conviction, either Warden
was required to seize the malefactor (if he could) and turn him over to the
corresponding Warden or, failing that, to provide sureties for him. In addition to these international tribunes, the Wardens all maintained courts
of their own for breaches of the Border laws within their own Marches.

It is impossible to set exact limits to the area which can be defined as
the Border Country; a sense of awareness of the Border is a matter of atmosphere rather than location. The Border to a Scotsman almost invariably means only the Scottish side, and the less patriotic and generally
less impressionable Englishman often accepts it to mean the same. Books
covering the Border written by Scotsmen frequently include places as far
away from the Border line as Peebles. But though situated on the unparalleled Tweed, among scenery as fine as any in the Borderland, it has
an atmosphere quite different, I feel, from that of Kelso or Jedburgh,
while Hexham, though nearly as far away from the frontier on the other
side, gives me the impression of being a real Border town. This con-
sciousness of the existence of the Border is probably owed to the fact that
Hexham was readily accessible to raiders from Scotland, through the long
but direct valley of the North Tyne, whereas to reach Peebles the English
had to cross several transverse valleys, so the Scottish town was able to
develop comparatively unmolested by the enemy's attentions.

The English side of the Border is not nearly so well known as the
Scottish side. There appear to be several reasons for the neglect of
Northumberland, in particular, by the traveller and holiday-maker. One,
no doubt, is the marked tendency of holiday travellers to move south and
west rather than north and east. Another is the comparative remoteness of
the county from large centres of population, though Northumberland is
less remote from these than, say, the popular Cornwall. A third reason
may be the climate, which is perhaps rather too bracing, except in the
height of summer, for the majority of tastes. But the principal factor,
without doubt, is the popular misconception that Northumberland is one
huge coalfield, a vast 'black country' littered with reeking slag-heaps, having no scenic beauty and nothing of historic interest. This impression may
be a relic of what we have been taught at school and, like too many impressions received during those formative years, it is one which many people never bother to confirm or deny. We learn to recite, parrot-fashion,
'the Northumberland and Durham coalfield'; we readily believe that these

counties are engulfed in a hugh black fog of coal dust and therefore can have little of interest or beauty to show. Nothing could be farther from the truth.

Of course, the coalfield is there, it cannot be denied. But in fact it covers no more than *one-twelfth* of Northumberland. In other words, if the coalfield were transferred to Warwickshire, it would encroach on that county to no greater extent in proportion than does Birmingham and its environs; if it were removed to Kent, it would cover no more of the 'Garden of England' than is already defaced by London and its sprawling suburbs. Yet no-one decries or ignores Warwickshire and Kent because they are partly despoiled by Birmingham and London.

Although the teeming industrial towns which hug the banks of the Tyne, together with (to some extent) the neighbouring coalfield, comprise one of the most densely inhabited areas of Britain, they are tucked away into one corner of Northumberland, and that part which is intrinsically the least interesting. The other eleven-twelfths of the county, extending up to the Border, remains one of the most sparsely populated areas in England. Northumberland ranks fifth in size among English counties, yet it is only seventeenth in the scale of population, and when we consider that the great majority of the inhabitants are concentrated in the industrial districts of Tyneside and the adjacent coalfield (more than one-third in Newcastle itself) the contrast in the distribution becomes apparent.

Most of Northumberland remains almost entirely unspoilt (outside the industrial area, no English county is less spoilt) and to a great extent in its natural state. To be convinced of this fact, one has only to travel by, say, the Newcastle to Jedburgh road over Carter Bar, part of a main trunk road to Edinburgh. Between Ponteland, about seven miles from Newcastle, and Jedburgh, nearly 50 miles on, only one collection of houses (Otterburn) can really justify the name of village. After the Highlander Inn, 3½ miles beyond Ponteland, no licensed house is met with until Otterburn is reached, 19 miles away, and from Byrness, 10 miles beyond Otterburn, no inn is passed before arriving at Jedburgh, over the Border and 16 miles on. Until recent years, no petrol pump was passed on the 21 miles between Rochester and Jedburgh. If it be argued that this is mainly hill country and such things as petrol pumps and even inns are not to be expected, one has in reply only to take any other main road to prove the assertion that Northumberland is practically an untouched county. On the road (A68) that follows the course of the Roman road of Dere Street between Corbridge and Elishaw (22 miles), no group of habitations can call itself a village, and on the Great North Road between Alnwick and Berwick-upon-Tweed (29 miles) only one place (Belford) is larger than a hamlet. And once off the main roads the truth of the assertion becomes even more evident.

Few parts of England are so fortunate, not only in their large areas of unspoilt natural scenery, but in the abundance and interest of their historic buildings and the wealth of their prehistoric remains. Apart from the pele towers, already mentioned, castles are the most important feature, as is only to be expected in a county so long engaged in the internecine strife of the Border. Some have been converted into splendid mansions; such castles as Alnwick, above the valley of the Aln where it is crossed by the Great North Road, and Bamburgh, rising from its precipitous rock on the wild sea-coast, can vie with the finest in any part of Britain. Other castles remain as imposing ruins, and of these Warkworth, above the lovely ravine of the Coquet, is the most complete, though Norham, on the Tweed, and Dunstanburgh, on the coast, are hardly less interesting, thanks partly to their magnificent situation.

Northumberland, too, as befits the county which can justly claim to be the birthplace of Christianity in northern England, is not without monastic buildings of charm and dignity. It is only necessary to mention Holy Island, still a goal of pilgrimage, with all its romantic connections with the see of Lindisfarne. The exquisite restored priory churches of Hexham and Brinkburn can compare with the better-known monasteries of Yorkshire, when beauty and not mere size is the measure. The delightfully-situated Hulne Priory was one of the two earliest foundations of the Carmelite Friars in Britain and is certainly the most important ruin of its kind.

The outstanding interest and beauty of the Northumbrian side of the Border has at last been recognised officially in the creation of the Northumberland National Park, an area of 398 square miles extending from Hadrian's Wall in the south to the Cheviot Hills. Information centres are to be found in the national park at Once Brewed, near the finest part of the Wall; at Byrness, in Redesdale, on the Carter Bar road; and at Ingram, in the Breamish Valley of the Cheviots. In addition, 50 square miles of the coast, from Amble, south of Warkworth, to a point just south of Berwick (and including Holy Island and the Farne Islands) have been designated an Area of Outstanding Beauty.

The Northumbrian himself is probably the most reserved of Englishmen, but this is not in the least surprising when we consider that for several centuries Northumberland was practically a cultural island, with the sea bounding one side of its long-sided triangle, the perpetual menace of the marauding Scot along the Border on another, and on the third a scarcely more sociable neighbour, the independent principality of the bishops of Durham, who as counts-palatine enjoyed rights of sovereignty over-riding those of the king himself within the boundaries of their possessions.

The initial impression of roughness which the Northumbrian often conveys to the stranger is, I think, largely the result of his brogue. Though to the Southerner the general effect of all North Country speech may be very much the same, to the ear attuned to the subtleties of dialect and intonation in the North there is a different language for each district. That of the farmers and shepherds of the Northumberland hill districts is certainly one of the most difficult to understand. Part of the difficulty is due to the unfamiliarity of the speech; it has not become hackneyed in the music-halls or found its way into the novel (Sir Walter Scott, in *Rob Roy*, makes his Northumbrians speak like Lowland Scots). The dialect is indeed hardly capable of being translated into the printed word, which is perhaps one of the reasons why the county has not produced a dialect poet of more than local reputation.

The Northumbrian countryman's speech is quite distinct from that of Tyneside, which, probably because it has been carried to other parts of the country (and has now been made familiar on television), is usually taken as the normal speech of the whole of the North-East. At the same time it has little in common with the delightful lilt, the carefully-mouthed vowels, the crisply-edged phrases of the Lowland Scot. A comparison with the Lowland Scottish dialect reveals that although a great similarity can be found between the dialect words (many of which betray their Anglian origin), the way in which the words are spoken differs very considerably. A possible reason for this is that when the words were first formed, both sides of the Border belonged to the great kingdom of Bernicia, but centuries of subsequent separation have resulted in the growth of two distinctly different dialects. The chief characteristic of the Northumbrian

Borderer's speech, apart from what may appear as a certain gruffness (due to the voice coming from low in the throat), is the 'burring' of the letter *r*, a sort of swallowing of the letter, so that a word like *brown* becomes (as near as can be written) *b(w)own*, *gather* becomes *gaathe(w)*, and so on.

For roughly one-quarter of its course the Border line bounds the county of Cumberland. Less is to be said about this part of the Border in proportion to its extent, simply because it is less important, both scenically and historically. Northumberland, cut off for centuries from the south, was forced by circumstances to face towards the Border, but North Cumberland has always looked in three directions, south-west to the Lake District and south-east to the Pennines (the hills of both regions thrust themselves on the eye from every point), as well as north towards Scotland.

Except for Bewcastle, with its Roman fort, its Edwardian castle and its singular Anglian cross, and the solitary (though beautiful) examples of medieval architecture in Naworth Castle and Lanercost Priory, the corner of Cumberland between the Irthing and the Esk conveys the impression of being a forgotten, a no-man's land. Few roads penetrate to its frontiers, and Sighty Crag, its highest point, rising to only 1701 feet, is in fact little more than a lift in the general waste of featureless moorland that spreads towards the Northumberland boundary (though these moorlands have now been encroached on by the plantations of the Kershope and Spadeadam Forests). That part of Hadrian's Wall which traversed Cumberland has largely disappeared, and the ancient Border city of Carlisle, though it can show some individual points of interest (in particular, its castle and cathedral), has grown into an industrial and commercial centre and has almost lost its medieval flavour.

A characteristic of the North Cumberland landscape is the frequent intrusion of the Old Red Sandstone, toning well with the richer greenery of the western zone of the Border. It makes itself felt in the local architecture; the exquisite priory of Lanercost, for example, is built of red sandstone, and the same warm-looking stone appears in the cathedral and castle of Carlisle. The country itself, surrounded by three ranges of hills of quite different formation, displays a succession of marked changes of scenery, from the empty moorland wastes on its eastern boundary, through the mild undulations of the central portion, split up by deeply-carved valleys, to the grassy alluvial flats, dissected by many creeks, that bound the shores of the Solway Firth.

Little need be said at this stage about the Scottish side of the Border, not of course because it is of less importance than the English side (an opinion no Scotsman would dream of subscribing to), but because, since the time of Sir Walter Scott (and partly due to his influence), it has been visited more often and described more frequently, and consequently is much better known. Agriculturally, it is richer than the English side of the Border, and scenically many will consider it superior. Some indeed, carried away perhaps by the eloquence of Scott, have found themselves disappointed with the scenery; Washington Irving, for one, viewed with 'mute surprise, I may almost say with disappointment', the 'mere succession of grey waving hills, line beyond line, as far as my eye could reach, monotonous in their aspect, and ... destitute of trees'. But the fault lies not with Scott; the 'Wizard of the North' not only knew the hills for themselves, he knew their exciting historic past and was able to people them with real and vivid characters. The occasional visitor, if not aware of this background, may fail to sense the romance and may feel in consequence that Scott has exaggerated.

To Alexander Geikie, that penetrating dissecter of the Scottish scene, the hills were anything but monotonous. 'Nowhere else in Scotland', he asserts in *The Scenery of Scotland*, 'can the exquisite modelling of flowing curves in hill-forms be so conspicuously seen. . . . From the skyline on either side, gentle but boldly-drawn curves of bent-covered moorland sweep down into the grassy meadow on the floor of the valley. These are architectural forms and remain distinct at all seasons of the year. But their beauty and impressiveness vary from month to month, almost from hour to hour.'

But what is it that makes the Borderland unique? Scenery as fine, or finer, may be found in other parts of England and Scotland. Its history is paralleled by that of the Welsh Border, which, too, has its splendid castles and beautiful abbeys. Lawlessness was as hard and as fearless there, and the raid and the foray were run as on the Scottish Border, though peace came 300 years earlier. What, then, is outstanding in the Scottish Border? 'It is this,' says G. M. Trevelyan in his charming essay on the Middle Marches, 'the Border people wrote the Border ballads. Like the Homeric Greeks, they were cruel, coarse savages, slaying each other as beasts of the forest; and yet they were also poets who could express in the grand style the inexorable fate of the individual man and woman, and infinite pity for all the cruel things which they none the less perpetually inflicted on one another. It was not one ballad maker alone but the whole cut-throat population who felt this magnanimous sorrow, and the consoling charm of the highest poetry. A large body of popular ballads commemorated real incidents of this wild life, or adapted folklore stories to the places and conditions of the Border. The songs so constructed on both sides of the Cheviot Ridge were handed down by oral tradition among the shepherds, and among the farm girls who, for centuries, sang them to each other at the milking. If the people had not loved the songs, many of the best would have perished. The Border Ballads, for good or for evil, express this society and its quality of mind, as well and as truly as the daily Press and the Music Hall Stage express that of the majority of town-dwellers of to-day.'

Occasions for getting some impressions of various aspects of Border life today are the Shepherds' Shows at Alwinton and Yetholm (described in Chapter 6), the Northumberland County Show in Hulne Park (Chapter 7), and the Cumberland County Show in Bitts Park at Carlisle (Chapter 14). On the Scottish side of the Border, agricultural shows take place at Kelso and Hawick (both in July) and at Langholm (in September). Shows are held also near Wooler (the Glendale Show), in August, and at Bellingham and Harbottle (both on a late Saturday in August). The Border Games take place at Jedburgh in July and the Whittingham Games and Fair are held in August. A Civic Week, with a historical pageant, concerts and other entertainments, is organised at Kelso during the third week in July; other occasions, commemorating historical events on the Scottish side, are referred to in Chapters 11 to 14.

The Border Country is traversed from south to north by the northernmost section of the Pennine Way, the walking route of over 250 miles established in 1965, mainly through the efforts of Tom Stephenson, doyen of ramblers, and extending from Edale, in the Peak District, to Kirk Yetholm, just over the Border, in Scotland.

The Pennine Way enters our region by crossing the Newcastle-Carlisle road west of Greenhead. It then bridges the Tipalt Burn near Thirlwall Castle (Chapter 2) and follows Hadrian's Wall east to a point a little short of Housesteads. From here the Way crosses the moors to the north and passes through Wark Forest (Chapter 3) to Bellingham. It goes on over the moors and up Redesdale (Chapter 4) to Byrness, on the Newcastle-Jedburgh road, then continues north to the Chew Green Roman forts (Chapter 5) near the Border line, which it follows for the rest of the way, over the Cheviot Hills (Chapter 6), before descending to Kirk Yetholm.

The popularity of the Pennine Way means that more walkers are getting to know at least part of the Border Country. For road travellers there are many ways of reaching the Border, whether from the English side or the Scottish. As an Englishman, approaching from the south, I have chosen to follow the Romans and begin by exploring the original frontier of Hadrian's Wall.

CHAPTER TWO

Hadrian's Wall

Recorded history in the Border, as indeed in the greater part of Britain, begins with the invasion of the Romans in the 1st century A.D. The armies of the Emperor Claudius, landing in Kent in the year 43, first established a base on the River Thames, then struck out in three directions: one to the west, one to the north-west towards Chester along the line of what became Watling Street, and a third to the north to Lincoln, later extended to York, which became the northern military headquarters. At that time most of what is now the North of England was occupied by a barbarous and turbulent people, the Brigantes, while south Scotland (as it is now) was divided up among a number of separate tribes which were later referred to collectively as the Picts.

The Roman conquest of the North began in about A.D. 73, but its most effective achievements coincided with the governorship of Julius Agricola (78–84), who carried the line of Watling Street through Chester (the north-west legionary headquarters) as far as Carlisle, where a fort was built, later to develop into the town of *Luguvalium*. At the same time another road (now called Dere Street) was constructed from York to the Tyne, where a second fort was established on the north bank of the river (Chapter 4), and the ends of these roads were connected by a third road called the Stanegate, built after A.D. 78 and defended from the barbarians farther north by a series of intermediate forts.

From the Tyne Agricola pushed on through wild and inhospitable country to gain the plain between the Forth and the Clyde, extending Dere Street and building a further line of forts. But early in the 2nd century (A.D. 117) the Brigantes rose successfully in revolt with the Picts, the recently-won Roman possessions were overrun, and the invaders retreated to a more easily defended frontier, stabilised along a line to the north of the Stanegate. By 122 the Emperor Hadrian himself had arrived to avenge the disastrous defeat; he decided to establish a defence zone here as the northernmost boundary of the Roman empire, and either he or the new governor of Britain, Aulus Platorius Nepos, planned and began the construction of the great wall that now bears the emperor's name.

The new frontier, between the Tyne and the Solway Firth, had the advantage of being both short and direct (across the narrowest part of England, in fact), of crossing in its middle and most difficult part some readily-defensible country, and of being much closer to the legionary headquarters at York and Chester. In addition, it could not conveniently be circumvented by sea; the inhospitable east coast itself effectively prevented any attempt in that direction, while along the flatter Cumberland coast for about 40 miles was built a series of supplementary fortifications.

The Wall was designed to link up a succession of independent forts, and, though altered several times in detail during building, was substantially finished by A.D. 130, apart from a section of the western zone, constructed in turf, yet remaining to be replaced in stone. As finally constituted, the complete military work, immense alike in conception and execution, comprised, in addition to the great Wall itself and its linking forts, (1) a broad ditch, following the wall on its northern side, (2) an intricate earthwork, called the Vallum, on the southern side and mostly at some distance from the Wall, and (3) a road, between the Wall and the Vallum, for the convenient transport of troops and equipment to supply or reinforce one part or another of the defences.

The Wall itself was almost 73 miles (80 Roman miles) long and stretched from Wallsend-on-Tyne to Bowness-on-Solway. It was faced on both sides with square blocks of stone, each of a size capable of being carried and placed in position by one man, without the help of cranes and other contrivances, and the core was composed of a mixture of rubble and mortar. The wall was mostly 8 Roman feet (about 7 feet 6 inches) thick, though originally it was intended to be 10 Roman feet thick throughout; foundations of this width were laid practically all the way from Newcastle to Willowford, beyond Gilsland on the Irthing, and a stretch of the wall itself at the eastern end was completed on this scale. Its height cannot now be ascertained exactly, since no part of it remains anything like complete, but the height to the sentry walk along its top was probably about 15 feet, and the walk was no doubt protected by a parapet which would bring the total height up to about 20 feet.

The forts which were part of the Wall defence system numbered 17 in all, including *Vindolanda* (Chesterholm) and Carvoran (near Greenhead), both of which lie to the south of the Wall and belonged to the previous, Stanegate, system of fortifications. The other forts were built after the Wall itself was complete (Chesters and Housesteads cover the sites of mile-castles) and they are placed at distances varying from $2\frac{1}{4}$ to as much as 8 miles apart (each individual position was determined by an advantageous situation). The forts can be divided roughly into two sizes, the smaller of about 3 to $3\frac{1}{2}$ acres suitable for a garrison of 500 infantry, and the larger of some 5 to $5\frac{1}{2}$ acres housing either 1,000 infantry or 500 cavalry. The complete garrison of the Wall consisted of about 8,000 troops. The largest of the forts (and the headquarters of the commander of the Wall forces) was at Stanwix (north of Carlisle) and covered over 9 acres; the smallest was Drumburgh (on the Solway), of less than 2 acres (the size of *Pons Aelius*, at Newcastle, is unknown, but it was a small fort).

Each fort, bounded by a wall 5 feet thick, was rectangular in plan and had rounded corners (the 'playing-card' shape); the longer sides in most forts lay north and south across the wall, but in some, because of the particular situation of the fort, they were placed parallel to the wall, as on the crag-top of Housesteads. The forts were sometimes wholly on the south side of the wall, as might be expected at first thought; most frequently they projected through the wall to the northern side and had a gate on that side. This arrangement was adopted to suit the system of warfare for which the soldiers were trained. The Roman method was not to cower behind the fortifications, waiting for their opponents to strike, but to sally forth to the attack, armed with their traditional weapons, the sword and the throwing-spear, and in the typical close square formation known as the phalanx. The wall was unsuitable, and was never intended, as a purely defensive work; its ramparts could not have been wide enough for the deployment of troops, it was accessible on the south side only at widely-spaced points, and it was not designed for the use of artillery, as it certainly would have been had the Romans intended to man it from end to end. The wall, in fact, constituted a sentry-walk between a series of signal stations, from which the boundary denoting the limit of the Roman empire could effectively be patrolled, and a protection to the road linking and supplying the individual military forts.

Inside each fort were the central headquarters building, with its colonnaded forecourt, large assembly hall, regimental chapel, and strong-room; a house for the commanding officer (who usually had his own bath-house); a hospital; barracks for the troops; stables (if it were a cavalry fort); storerooms, workshops and offices; and granaries containing sufficient foodstuff to enable the garrison to withstand a siege for as long as a year. All the buildings were constructed of stone. Each fort had at least one gate (with guard chambers) in each wall, and sometimes two in the longer sides. Outside the fort were the inevitable bath-house, which with the Romans served also the function of a club, and a subsidiary village, where lived the wives and families of the garrison, trading people and the like, and native settlers, whom a strict discipline rigidly excluded (until after A.D. 367) from the confines of the fort itself.

In addition to these main forts, the Wall was strengthened by small intermediate forts at regular intervals, known as mile-castles and turrets. The mile-castles, so called because they were placed one Roman mile (about 1,620 yards) apart, as far as the ground permitted, were all attached to the south side of the wall and measured about 60 to 75 feet by about 50 to 65 feet. Each was provided with two gates; the north gate, opening through the wall, was surmounted by an observation-tower from which the sentry could look out across the barren wastes beyond. Inside each mile-castle were barracks for the garrison (of some 30 to 50 men), but there was little room for anything else. The length of the wall between each mile-castle was divided into three equal sections by two turrets, and each mile-castle was consequently responsible for the provisioning of one turret on each side of it. The turrets were about 20 feet square, slightly recessed into the south face of the wall, and entered by a doorway on the south side only. It is thought that the top of each turret projected above the wall to form a watch-tower; each would be manned by four men, two on duty on the wall itself, while the other two rested within the turret.

The military road, which was about 16 feet wide and had a hard gravel surface, kept close behind the wall and joined up the forts. It usually ran straight through these, entering and leaving by a gate, and branches from it provided ready access to the mile-castles and turrets. The ditch following the wall on its northern side was V-shaped in section; it averaged 27 feet wide and 9 feet deep, with its inner edge usually about 20 feet away from the wall, leaving a flat space between them. No ditch, of course, was necessary where the ground fell away steeply from the wall, as for instance where this crosses the great upstanding crags at Housesteads and Crag Lough.

The Vallum, the last of the works to be described, was the last to be constructed to complete the zone of fortification. Originally it consisted merely of a flat-bottomed ditch, 20 feet across at the top and 10 feet deep. The earth thrown out in excavating this was arranged in two continuous ramparts or mounds each about 20 feet wide at the base and about 6 feet high, set back 30 feet on each side from the edge of the ditch. The Vallum then served to exclude unauthorised persons from the frontier zone. Later, during the reign of Antoninus Pius, the ditch was filled in at intervals of about 45 yards to form a series of causeways (the only surviving example can be seen at Benwell, west of Newcastle) and gaps were cut in the mounds on either side to provide a way through these, so that the Wall and the road in front of it were readily accessible from the south. In the 3rd century much of the ditch was cleared out again and the causeways removed, and the earth then excavated was deposited on the edge of the ditch, usually on the southern side, so that in crossing the Vallum from south to north we find, in most places, mound, space, mound, ditch, space, mound, the two outer mounds having gaps in them at fairly regular intervals. Like the Wall, the Vallum was in no sense a defence work; its purpose was not to keep out the Brigantes at all costs, and it was throughout its existence crossed by permanent causeways (though protected by gateways) at the forts and mile-castles.

The building of the Wall was substantially carried out by the three Roman legions then in Britain (the 2nd, the 6th and the 20th), assisted in at least the rougher labour by the native Britons, whose tribal organisation, by no means primitive (as is often thought), was acknowledged by the invaders. Each Roman century (in practice, about 80 men) built a certain length of the Wall (about 50 yards) and often recorded the event, happily for the historian, by an inscription, then moved to a similar length farther along. Subsequent repairs were often undertaken by British tribes under the direction of Roman officers.

The Wall defences were hardly completed before a new policy was put into operation. Antoninus Pius, successor to Hadrian, decided to push the frontier forward, and his governor, Lollius Urbicus, struck through the Border Country and established a new boundary by building (in about A.D. 143) a wall between the Forth and the Clyde, partly along a line of forts already created by Agricola, and much of the garrison was moved northward to police it. The Antonine Wall resembled Hadrian's fortification to some extent (except that it was of turf or clay instead of stone). The Brigantes, taking advantage of this weakening of the defences of the North and the fact that the supply lines from the legionary bases at York and Chester were once again extended, rose in revolt and in about 155 inflicted on the Romans a great defeat which was saved from being a disaster only by the intervention of reinforcements under a new governor, Julius Verus.

The Romans were defeated again in about 181, this time by the northern Caledonians, and the wall of Antoninus was greatly damaged; and after another new governor of Britain, Clodius Albinus, had been routed in Gaul while making a claim to the imperial throne, the whole of the Roman possessions north of York and Chester were devastated by the native tribes and both walls were effectively wrecked. Septimius Severus, the victorious emperor, himself crossed the Channel (in 208) and though he was so old and ailing that he had to be carried in a litter, he superintended the repair of Hadrian's Wall and re-established it as the frontier. So well was the work carried out, in fact, that for centuries the original building of the Wall was confidently assigned to him. Britain thenceforth enjoyed nearly a century of peace, but towards the end of the 3rd century serious disturbances broke out once more. The repaired Wall was often breached, particularly during a great uprising of the Picts, the Scots and a new enemy, the Saxons, acting together in 367, and by this time the garrison was being sadly depleted to fend off the Saxon pirates who were raiding the southern coasts. The Wall held out until 383, when Magnus Maximus took the best part of the garrison to assist his bid for the title of emperor. He was defeated and killed, and there is no evidence that the Wall was ever re-garrisoned. Early in the 5th century, the whole of the Roman forces in Britain were finally withdrawn.

Though a few fragments of the Wall can be seen east of north Tynedale (at Heddon-on-the-Wall and Denton Burn), by far the most important lengths now upstanding lie between Chollerford, where the Wall crossed the North Tyne, and Banks, near Brampton, in Cumberland, though the Vallum is still visible throughout most of its course. The eastern end of the Wall was intentionally destroyed. During the Jacobite revolt of 1745 the Government forces under General Wade were at Newcastle when Prince Charles Edward, altering his plans, struck across country from Kelso to Carlisle. Owing to the lack of an adequate road, Wade was unable to move his artillery over to the west to stop him. After the suppression of the rising a new road (now referred to as the Military Road) was ordered to be built. To facilitate its construction, the Wall was cast down for the best part of a distance of nearly 28 miles from Newcastle, and the road was carried on its foundations. But from a point east of Sewingshields Farm the Military Road leaves the Wall (which continues over the tops of a succession of basaltic crags, a setting of wild and impressive grandeur) and follows it at no very great distance on its southern side.

This centre section of the Wall (by far the finest part) is most adequately explored on foot, though various points on it may be reached from the Military Road. The most interesting places to visit are Chesters (just to the west of Chollerford), Housesteads (about midway between Chollerford and Gilsland, on the Irthing) and Chesterholm, the fort of *Vindolanda*, on the Stanegate. Those who have been led to expect a great deal of the Wall may be a little disappointed at first sight. Both forts and wall have served as a convenient quarry for centuries; even where the wall has not disappeared entirely, its height has been reduced to 5 or 6 feet, and the forts mostly show little more than foundations. Many stones (some with inscriptions) have been built into the houses and walls of the neighbourhood. A smattering of history and the eye of imagination are required to appreciate the Wall to the full.

To the east of Chollerford little of interest is to be seen (though the excavation of the terminal fort at Wallsend, on the Tyne, began in 1975). The Military Road, after leaving the main road from Newcastle to Carlisle at Heddon-on-the-Wall, climbs over open, undulating country, with widening views. Earthworks at Halton Chesters indicate the site of the fort of *Onnum* (or *Hunnum*), and at Stagshawbank (Chapter 4), three-quarters of a mile farther, the line of the Wall crosses the Roman Dere Street, along which, $2\frac{1}{2}$ miles south, is the supply base of *Corstopitum*. To the north of the Military Road, 3 miles farther on, and at the edge of a hill overlooking North Tynedale, is the small chapel of St Oswald, built in 1737, traditionally near the site of the Battle of Heavenfield, in which Oswald, King of Northumbria (afterwards St Oswald), defeated the pagan King Cadwalla of Wales in 635, a major step in the establishment of Christianity in England. A large wooden cross by the roadside resembles that set up by Oswald before the battle, as recounted by Bede in his *Ecclesiastical History*. At Planetrees, farther on, a short length of the wall was saved from destruction in 1801 through the intervention of William Hutton, the historian, who at the age of 78 walked from Birmingham to Carlisle, along the Wall to Wallsend, back to Carlisle and then home to Birmingham, a distance of over 600 miles! Beyond Planetrees the Military Road, bearing north from the line of the Wall, descends steeply into the dale, crossing the Hexham–Rothbury road. Along this, towards Hexham, can be seen a section of the Wall with an excellent example of a turret.

On the east bank of the North Tyne, half a mile below the ridge over the river at Chollerford (Chapter 3), we can see an abutment of the bridge which carried the Roman military way across; a change in the course of the river has left it high and dry. The western abutment, now almost in midstream, can be seen when the water is low. On a shelf above this side of the river, in the fine park of Chesters, are the important remains of *Cilurnum*, where the arrangements of a Roman cavalry fort may be studied better than anywhere else. Still to be seen are the gateways, with their guard chambers; the lower courses of the long barracks; the impressive headquarters building, with the usual courtyard, covered hall and other apartments, and an underground strong-room; and the commanding officer's house and his private bath-house, under which are the pillared hypocausts through which hot air was passed for heating the rooms above. The fort lay almost as much to the north of the Wall as to the south, and of its six gates three open on the north side of the Wall, so that the troops could get out easily and quickly to deal with an attacker. Discovery of the remains of the wall and also a turret below ground prove that *Cilurnum* was built after the Wall itself was complete. Outside the fort on the south lay a civil settlement, which still awaits excavation; and down the slope towards the river are the large and well-preserved remains of the public bath-house (which resembled a Turkish bath in its arrangements), the finest example of a military bath-house in England. Near the park gates is a museum with an excellent collection of antiquities from *Cilurnum* and the Wall, including numerous milestones, altars, statues, inscribed tablets, tools and coins. Perhaps the most interesting objects are a beautifully-wrought corn-measure and the facsimile of a diploma, the official tablet presented to a native auxiliary soldier on his discharge from the army, granting him all the rights of a full Roman citizen. The eighteenth-century house of Chesters, the home of John Clayton, the antiquary who began the excavation of *Cilurnum* (in 1843), was much enlarged and altered by R. Norman Shaw in 1891.

To the west of Chesters the road (entering the Northumberland National Park) runs uphill out of the valley, mostly on the Wall foundations once more, but near Black Carts Farm a stretch of the wall, with a turret, can be seen to the north of the road. At Limestone Corner, which affords a wide view northward over North Tynedale to the Simonside and Cheviot Hills, both Vallum and ditch are cut through the solid basaltic rock. Farther on are the earthworks of Carrawburgh (pronounced '-bruff'), the Roman *Brocolitia*, lying south of the road (and of the Wall); it was added to the Wall defences after A.D. 130, and so was built after the Vallum, which it obliterates. To the south-west are the excavated remains, revealed in 1950, of a 3rd-century Temple of Mithras, a sun-god of Persian provenance who came to be worshipped throughout the Roman empire from the 1st century onward and was specially venerated by soldiers, officials and merchants. Mithraism was a personal religion for men only, with progressive grades of initiation, to which admission could be gained only through a series of rigorous ordeals. The temple had a nave separated on either side from narrow aisles by arcades (supported by sleeper walls) and a series of altars was placed at the inner end. It resembled that discovered in the City of London, and a reconstruction can be seen in the Museum of Antiquities in Newcastle University. To the west of the fort is the sacred well of the water-goddess Coventina; when this was cleaned out numerous coins, sculptures and votive offerings were found, some dating from a period after the official conversion of Rome to Christianity, early in the 4th century.

Before reaching the farm of Sewingshields, the Military Road turns southward from the course of the Wall, which climbs to the top of Sewingshields Crags (1069 feet), with a magnificent view of the wild and desolate moorlands stretching away towards the Border forests and of the Wall pushing ahead over the crests of the basaltic precipices of the Great Whin Sill. To the north-east is the dark mass of Cheviot; to the south-west is the soaring height of Cross Fell, the highest point in the Pennines; to the south-east one looks down the wooded South Tynedale towards Hexham. From the west end of the crag Broomlee Lough (pronounced 'luff'), one of the group of small and lonely Northumbrian lakes, comes into view.

The Wall is at its finest on either side of Housesteads (*Vercovicium*), which itself is the most completely excavated infantry fort on the Wall, as well as being the most splendidly situated. It lies wholly on the south side of the Wall, which here runs along the top of a precipitous crag, and its longer sides are arranged east and west, the better to suit the slope of the ground. Housesteads, together with a long stretch of the Wall on both sides, is the property of the National Trust; the layout can be studied on a plan and a model in the museum close by the farm. The arrangements were similar to those at *Cilurnum*, but the remains of the headquarters building, the long granaries, the barrack blocks and the four gateways are particularly well preserved, as are the angle towers and a latrine (an un-usual survival) at the south-east corner. In the 4th century Housesteads developed into a market centre and the gate on the north, which was ap-proached up the steep slope by a ramp, was inserted for the benefit of traders from that direction. To the east of the fort the Knag Burn penetrates the Wall by means of a culvert, and close by are remains of a gateway. Outside the fort on the south are distinctive cultivation terraces and traces of a civil settlement; the Vallum passes along the slope, which was once strewn with the relics of the worship of those many cults and religions that grew up round every Roman settlement.

To the west of Housesteads is an exceptionally well-preserved example of a mile-castle, with gates and barracks, and beyond this, at Rapishaw Gap in Cuddy's Crags (i.e. St Cuthbert's), the Pennine Way, coming from the west, goes off northward towards the plantations of Wark Forest (Chapter 3). Farther on, from the side of Hotbank Crags (1074 feet), a charming view is revealed of Crag Lough, a sombre lake lying right under the shadow of the Wall, below a tree-topped outcrop favoured by rock-climbers. The Wall continues over Peel Crags to the car park at Steel Rigg, from which we could walk back along the top of it, with a fine view of the lough. Farm roads to the north give access to Greenlee Lough, the largest of the Northumbrian lakes (1 mile long) and now a favourite place for sailing. The lane from Steel Rigg descends to the Military Road at the youth hostel and National Park information centre of Once Brewed. The Twice Brewed Inn, near by, once had a reputation akin to that of Mumps Ha' in Scott's *Guy Mannering*.

To the south-east of Once Brewed and about half a mile south of the Wall is *Vindolanda*, originally one of the line of forts along the Stanegate, occupied in A.D. 80–122 and again from about 163 to the 4th century. It can be approached on east or west from the modern (but little used) road which lies mainly on the site of the Roman road. To the west of the fort itself is the *vicus* or civil settlement, now under excavation by the Vindolanda Trust, formed in 1970 with this object. The buildings already revealed include a *mansio* or hostelry for travellers; the large 'Corridor House', perhaps the dwelling of a merchant or retired officer; and the married quarters of about 16 families of the soldiers. To the north of these buildings is the bath-house, built by the 6th Legion and used by both military and civilians, with the pillars of a hypocaust.

To the south of these excavations are reconstructions, made with the help of Gateshead schoolchildren, consisting of a length of the 'broad' stone wall (10 feet wide) with a turret and the outer ditch, and a length of turf wall (like that of the western part of Hadrian's Wall), with a timber mile-castle gateway. To the east of these is a section of the original turf and timber wall of the settlement, and to the west is a mausoleum with a central burial chamber. The fort itself, the last of six on the site, was reconstructed towards the end of the 3rd century and partly overlay the civil settlement. The headquarters building in the centre, occupied until after 374, has been excavated, and on the west side is a gate approached by a flagged road. On the other side of the Brackies Burn is the house of Chesterholm, built in 1831 and now the headquarters of the Trust, with a museum containing writing tablets, textiles and other finds made in the first military settlement which lay below the civil settlement. Near the burn, to the north, a Roman milestone still stands in its original position, beside the course of the Stanegate. On Barcombe Hill, to the east, is the site of a Roman signal station.

To the west of Steel Rigg, the course of Hadrian's Wall lifts to reach its greatest elevation at Winshields Crag (1230 feet), and from here the shining estuary of the Solway Firth can sometimes be seen ahead, in the evening light. The Wall continues along the Great Whin Sill to the well-preserved mile-castle of Cawfields, but beyond this it has been destroyed by a large quarry, where the upstanding strata of the Sill are well seen. From the Haltwhistle Burn the Wall (less well preserved in this section) goes on by way of Great Chesters (*Aesica*), one of the smallest of the forts (despite its modern name); it was supplied with water from the Caw Burn by a winding aqueduct about 3 miles long. A fine section of the Wall can be seen at Walltown, farther west, with a turret incorporating a signal tower built before the Wall. It then traverses the broken basalt crags known as the Nine Nicks of Thirlwall, at the west end of which is the site of the fort of Carvoran (perhaps named *Magnis* or *Banna*), detached from and well south of the Wall. It was not one of the Wall series, as already mentioned, but belonged to the Stanegate period (though restored in about 136), and it is separated from the Wall by the Vallum.

The Wall, leaving the high moorland country, takes a steep course down to the Tipalt Burn, where it is overlooked by the ruins of Thirlwall Castle, a fourteenth-century pele tower at the point where the Scots on some occasion 'thirled' (i.e. pierced) the Wall. A footbridge gives access to a road from Greenhead, a hamlet placed where the Military Road rejoins the main road to Carlisle. Our road, keeping to the north of the Wall, leads west to Gilsland, which once had some reputation as a small spa and angling resort, on the banks of the Irthing, among pleasant undulating country. It was while staying at Wardrew (a house of 1752, since altered), a mile upstream, that Walter Scott in 1797 met his future wife, Charlotte Charpentier, and he has described the surrounding countryside in *Guy Mannering*. The supposed original of the celebrated alehouse in the novel, where Meg of Mumps Ha' secreted freebooters who set upon travellers after they had left the inn and forthwith relieved them of their valuables (and sometimes their lives), has been located in Gilsland. The Irthing, which winds through beautiful woodlands, both above and below the village, rises on the Bewcastle Fells to the north, in a setting of extreme desolation.

Crossing the little Poltross Burn, south of the village, the Wall enters Cumberland. Near the burn is a good example of a mile-castle, and to the west, in the garden of the former vicarage, an interesting length of the broad wall foundation has been revealed, with the narrow wall on top of it. Farther west, another fine stretch of the Wall, with two turrets, leads down to the farm of Willowford, beyond which the Roman military way crossed the Irthing by a bridge, an abutment of which has been stranded in a field since the river changed its course.

On the top of Harrow's Scar, beyond the Irthing, is another mile-castle, and from this yet another impressive stretch of the Wall goes on to the farm of Birdoswald, adjoining the fort of *Camboglanna*, one of the largest on the Wall. It can be reached only by the road from Gilsland on the north side of the river. The fort resembled *Cilurnum* in design, except that it lies wholly on the south side of the wall; it has been excavated, but disappointingly little is now to be seen. From the south-west corner we have an enchanting view over the Irthing valley to the distant Skiddaw and Saddleback. The course of a Roman road, the northward extension of the Maiden Way, can be traced across the lonely moors to Bewcastle (Chapter 15).

To the west of Harrow's Scar the Wall was originally constructed of turves (mainly because limestone was not available locally for use as cement). They were arranged in parallel courses, and the mile-castles were also turf-walled, though the turrets were built of stone. Later in the 2nd century, the turf wall was replaced by one of stone, but between Birdoswald and Wallbowers ($1\frac{1}{2}$ miles west), the stone wall took a more northerly course than the turf, so the turf wall remained in view, except where it was obliterated by *Camboglanna*. The line of this wall can be traced, though the turves have long since consolidated in a clayey mass. At Pike Hill, a mile west of Wallbowers, is an unusual signalling tower, built earlier than the Wall but later incorporated in its structure.

Before reaching the hill-top hamlet of Banks (locally, The Banks), farther on, a good specimen of a turret is passed; and at Hare Hill, beyond the Banks Burn, is the highest piece of wall (about 10 feet) now remaining. But from here to the western extremity of the Wall at Bowness there is very little to see and its course is not worth tracing, especially as the country, too, is less attractive. From Banks the interest changes to the medieval buildings of Lanercost Priory and Naworth Castle (Chapter 15) and to the old town of Brampton on the road to Carlisle.

CHAPTER THREE

Hexham and North Tynedale

Hexham, one of the oldest market towns in the Border and the unofficial capital of Tynedale, stands on the south bank of the river scarcely 2 miles below the junction of its two long branches. The South Tyne, rising on the Pennine moors not far from Cross Fell, and flowing first north past Alston, then due east by Haltwhistle and Haydon Bridge, runs through country that is not typical of the Border and is therefore outside the scope of this book. But the North Tyne has its source right on the Border line and flows through a valley which shows many signs that it was familiar with the Scottish raiders, who hurried down it on frequent occasions, attracted by the rich pastureland of lower Tynedale.

The first impression of Hexham is that of the quiet dignity of a small cathedral city. The main Newcastle to Carlisle road passes through the town by a long rising street that bears the names of Priestpopple, Battle Hill and Hencotes in succession. But the old town centre is isolated to the north of this, and its narrow streets are mostly grouped around the wide market place, on one side of which rises the graceful priory church, itself larger and more impressive than some cathedrals. Behind this and along the river are parks with a profusion of trees unusual in a Border town. But the feeling of peace is dispelled and the rough life of the past is brought crowding back as one turns across the market place, with its roofed and pillared market house of 1766, to confront the grim, dark, massive walls of the Moot Hall, from 1112 until 1545 the tower-house of the bailiff of the Archbishop of York, who was lord of the Regality of Hexham. Restored in 1355, it is now the public library. Behind the Moot Hall is the Manor Office, the prison of the regality, the only one of its kind and the first official prison in England. Built in 1332, it was in use as a place of confinement until 1824.

The known history of Hexham can be traced back to the Saxons, who gave it the name of *Hagustaldes ea* (perhaps the 'warrior's stream'), but by Norman times this had been changed to Hextoldesham. In about 674, St Wilfrid, then Bishop of York, the prototype of the haughty and ambitious churchman met with again in the persons of Bek and Wolsey, laid the foundations of a splendid church that 'of all others throughout England . . . was deemed the first for workmanship, design and unequalled beauty'. The church was in the tradition of the Roman school of builders which Wilfrid, himself under the Roman influence, passed on to English craftsmen, and it was, according to Eddius, the chronicler of the bishop, without rival in size and magnificence north of the Alps.

Of this great building, practically all that now remains is the crypt, which resembles that under Ripon Cathedral (also built for Wilfrid) and is one of the few Saxon crypts surviving in England. It has a central chamber for the exhibition of relics (like Ripon) and it is built largely of Roman stones from *Corstopitum*, one of which (unique in Britain) bears an inscription from which the name of the Emperor Geta was erased in A.D. 212, in accordance with an edict issued after his murder by his brother, previously joint ruler with him. Another survival of the Roman occupation of Britain is the fine monument in the south transept to Flavinus, a standard-bearer, with a spirited representation of a Roman soldier riding down a prostrate Briton.

In 681 Hexham became the seat of a bishop by the division of the large diocese of Lindisfarne, which at that time stretched from the Tees to the Forth. The work of Wilfrid was continued by Acca, who died in about 740 and is commemorated in the church by a tall stone shaft carved with a double vine-scroll. Hexham remained the cathedral until 821, when the bishopric was re-absorbed into the diocese of Lindisfarne. Its most famous bishop, apart from Wilfrid, was John of Beverley, who built a monastery at that place on the site now occupied by the famous minster.

The Saxon church of Hexham was destroyed by the marauding Danes in 875 and its site lay desolate until about 1175, when a new priory church began to arise from the ruins, incorporating what survived of the Saxon work. The priory was settled in about 1113 by Augustinian canons, to whom is due the very beautiful choir and transepts, a 'text book of Early English architecture'. The transepts are remarkable for their great overall length in proportion to the nave and choir, for the grace of their arcaded and galleried walls and of the tall columns supporting the tower, and for the very unusual survival of the stairs, well worn through long use, by which the canons descended each night from their dormitory to the church for prayer and meditation. The priory had the right of giving sanctuary, and in the choir is a Bishop's Chair or Frithstool, probably of the 7th or 8th century, which was used in the Middle Ages as a sanctuary stool. In the south choir aisle is preserved a rare 7th-century chalice.

The choir has fifteenth-century stalls with carved misericords (brackets under the seats) and paintings of seven bishops of Hexham, below which (on the north side) are four scenes from a remarkable 'Dance of Death', a medieval morality painting with representations of Cardinal, King, Bishop and Pope. The choir is flanked by the small fifteenth-century Ogle and Leschman Chantries, and behind the latter (on the north) are some curious figures carved in stone, including a Northumbrian bagpipe player. The Northumbrian small pipes, played only in this county, differ from the familiar Scottish pipes principally in that they are carried under the arm (the wind-bag being filled by bellows operated by the arm instead of being blown up by the mouth) and they have a sweeter, less strident, tone. (The Duke of Northumberland still retains his own piper at Alnwick Castle, as he has done since 1756.)

The choir is separated from the crossing by an exquisite early sixteenth-century pulpitum, a carved wooden screen whose painted panels, effaced at the Reformation, have since been restored. The priory was attacked several times by the Scots; the nave and the east end of the choir were completely destroyed by them in 1296 and seem not to have been restored afterwards. The east end was rebuilt in 1858 by John Dobson, the Newcastle architect, who modelled it on the style of that of Whitby Abbey, but the nave remained in a ruinous condition until 1908, when it was restored in the Decorated style to the design of Temple Moore. Externally, the church, apart from its sturdy but harmonious tower, suffers somewhat from the lack of concord between the rather stark newness of its more recent masonry and the older stonework, much of the detail of which has been obliterated by the hand of time and the inclement northern climate. But the interior will bear close comparison with any other large church in the country. To the south of the church are some remains of the domestic buildings of the priory, and near Market Street, to the north-west, are ruins of the late twelfth-century gatehouse.

From Hexham roads run up both sides of the beautiful North Tynedale, which is outstanding among Border valleys in being well wooded for a large part of its course; in fact, until beyond Wark there are few glimpses of the desolate moorlands that lie back from the valley on either side. One road crosses the Tyne by the graceful bridge built in 1788 by Robert Mylne, then ascends the east bank of the North Tyne, through Wall, a pleasant village built round a spacious green, before crossing the line of Hadrian's Wall above Chollerford (Chapter 2).

The road on the west side of the North Tyne gives the better views. Leaving the road which pushes through the Tyne Gap towards Carlisle, it crosses the South Tyne to Warden, a hamlet in the angle between the two rivers. The church has an eleventh-century tower (with Roman jambs to the arch) and thirteenth-century transepts, but the rest was rebuilt in 1765 with stones brought from Hadrian's Wall. The road goes on across the side of Warden Law (593 feet), the top of which, capped by the ramparts of an Iron Age hill-fort (now much denuded), commands extensive views up the valleys of both North and South Tyne. Crossing the line of the Wall, we meet the Military Road, which runs east past Chesters (Chapter 2) to the George Inn at Chollerford, beside the bold bridge built after 1771 over a placid reach of the North Tyne.

A by-road continues on the west bank to Humshaugh (the second syllable is pronounced '-half') and then to Haughton Castle (pronounced 'How-ton'), a building partly of the thirteenth and fourteenth centuries. This stronghold of the Swinburnes and later the Widdringtons was greatly extended and altered in 1876, by Anthony Salvin, and again later, but it preserves as fine an example of a single tower-house as any in the Border. Haughton, like many a Border hold, has its grim story of the medieval unrest. It concerns Archie Armstrong, one of the infamous Liddesdale troopers, who had been captured by Sir Thomas Swinburne and confined to a deep dungeon. Sir Thomas then set out on a long journey and had got as far as York, it is said, before he remembered that no instructions had been left for feeding the prisoner. A hurried return to Haughton, however, brought him back too late; Armstrong was already dead, the flesh knawed from his arms as he succumbed to the agony of hunger.

Beyond the castle, we join the main road on the west of the North Tyne and skirt the grounds of Nunwick Hall. The house, hidden among its trees (which include some beeches, not native to Northumberland), is a fine building of 1752, altered in about 1829 by Joseph Bonomi, the Durham architect. Roads on the left lead to the secluded hamlet of Simonburn, with white-washed cottages strewn round a green. The fourteenth-century church was partly rebuilt in 1763 by Robert and William Newton, but altered again in 1864–77. The parish, once the largest in the Border, stretched away over country of extreme desolation to the boundaries of Cumberland and Roxburghshire. The hamlet stands above the Crook Burn, which may be followed upstream towards Tecket Linn, a pretty cascade in a charming little ravine.

From the main road, farther on, we can look across the river to Chipchase Castle, consisting of a mansion of 1621, 'the finest example of Jacobean architecture in Northumberland', built on to a fourteenth-century pele tower; both were homes of the Herons, the official keepers of Tynedale. Standing solitary in the park is a chapel of about 1740 which still retains its original fittings.

Our road goes on to Wark-on-Tyne, pleasantly situated in a richly wooded part of the dale. At the entrance to the village is a steep-sided motte-hill, of the kind we shall see also at Elsdon and Wark-on-Tweed (from these, in fact, the two Warks take their name). It was part of a stronghold of the Norman 'motte-and-bailey' type which subsequently grew into the most important castle in Tynedale. The whole of Northumberland had been ceded to David I of Scotland by Stephen in 1139, and though the county was regained by Henry II in 1157, Tynedale (the name included the valleys of both North and South Tyne) was granted to William the Lion in 1159 and continued under Scottish jurisdiction until forfeited by John Baliol in 1296. During this later period, at least, Wark was the capital of the regality of Tynedale and from the castle hall justice was dispensed, but all traces of the hall have now disappeared. When Robert Bruce raided the North of England in 1314, after his resounding victory at Bannockburn, he resumed the lordship of the regality and the men of Tynedale paid homage to him. The farmhouse now crowning the motte was formerly a manor house of the Radcliffes, later Earls of Derwentwater, but was forfeited with others of that family's estates after the Jacobite débâcle of 1715.

Quiet upland roads running west from Wark will take us to Stonehaugh, one of the new villages created by the Forestry Commission for the workers in their vast holdings in Northumberland (about which more will be said below). The village, beside the delightful Warks Burn, serves the Wark Forest, which covers a region of once bleak and rather barren moorland. The forest is traversed from south to north by the Pennine Way on its route from Hadrian's Wall (near Housesteads) to Bellingham. The remarkable 'totem poles' beside the burn at Stonehaugh were carved by forest workers.

From the Houxty Burn, north of Wark, the main road climbs away from the river, which is joined down to the east by the Rede, coming through Redesdale (Chapter 4), among a rich profusion of woods. Beyond the crest of the ridge the grey roofs of Bellingham (pronounced 'Bel-lin-jam'), the market centre for North Tynedale, are seen stretched out below, in an open part of the dale, and the road descends to it. The town still conveys the aloof atmosphere of a place for so long near a disputed frontier, and it requires little imagination to visualise, even today, the Scottish raiders riding over the moor or down the long dale. This aspect is reflected nowhere more than in the towerless church, first built in the thirteenth century and looking out over the river. The thick walls, heavily buttressed, the small windows, widely splayed inside, and the massive roofs of stone slabs on the nave and transept, supported by barrel vaults with stout stone ribs, all point to the possibility of its use for defence, though in fact the nave and transept were rebuilt after the Union of the Crowns in 1603. The new work indeed is in a style that is distinctively Scottish. Churches in England which have complete stone roofs integral with the rest of the building are to be found only in the Border counties. At Bellingham the ribs of the ceiling vault actually merge into the walls.

Cut into the moors to the north of the town is a wooded cleugh or ravine and the path through this (now a nature trail) leads to the delightful little waterfall of Hareshaw Linn. The Pennine Way, coming from the Warks Burn through an upland pastoral region of many farmsteads, joins the road from Wark a mile before it crosses the North Tyne to Bellingham. From the town the Way goes on northward by Blakelaw and Hareshaw House, then over rather featureless moorland to Lord's Shaw (1167 feet), with a forward view to the Cheviot Hills. 'Shaw' means a wood in the Border, indicating that this region was once well wooded. The route continues over Padon Hill (1240 feet), on the top of which is an obelisk to Alexander Peden, the Scottish Covenanter (who came over the Border to hold religious meetings here), then descends through the forest into Redesdale.

From Bellingham, roads run up both sides of the North Tyne, taking us into the Northumberland National Park. The peaceful green and well-timbered reaches of the lower part of the dale have given way to more open and wilder country, and the many ruined tower-houses in this district are evidence of the lawlessness of former times. Some indeed were first built when Tynedale came under Scottish administration, and Scottish nobles moved in to occupy new lands. Grassy mounds are all that remain of Tarset Castle, built in 1267 by John Comyn, father of the 'Red Comyn' whose murder in the Greyfriars church at Dumfries in 1306 stirred up so much trouble in Scotland. The road going on from here crosses the Tarset Burn, which flows down through a once-lonely moorland region (now partly afforested) whose inhabitants in the Middle Ages had a reputation for lawlessness akin to that of Redesdale not far away. At Gatehouse, above the junction of its tributary the Tarret Burn, are two good examples of pele towers.

The more interesting road from Bellingham on the south of the North Tyne passes Hesleyside, a fine house mostly of the eighteenth century and partly by William Newton. It is still the seat of the Charltons of Charlton, an ancient Northumbrian family who distinguished themselves in the Border wars. Tradition has it that when the larder was empty, the lady of the Charltons served a spur on a dish for dinner, as a hint to her master that he must 'ride and reive' over the Border to secure the next meal. The grounds were laid out by Lancelot 'Capability' Brown, the most famous landscape gardener, who was born in 1716 at Kirkharle, near the Newcastle-Otterburn road.

A by-road farther on ascends the valley of the Chirdon Burn, passing Dally Castle, one of the earliest of the pele towers, built by David Lindsay in about 1237 but now consisting mainly of earthworks. The road ends beyond the farm of Bower, but forest ways go on towards the Seven Linns, a series of cascades through twisting rocky gorges, best seen when the burn is in spate. The North Tynedale road passes the isolated church of Greystead, built in 1818 when the Commissioners of Greenwich

Hospital, who held the living, decided to divide the huge and un-manageable parish of Simonburn into smaller parishes. As a result other churches were built at Wark and Humshaugh and at Thorneyburn near the Tarset Burn.

Beyond the small village of Falstone we leave the National Park as we reach the boundary of the Forestry Commission's vast holdings in the Border Country. The adjoining forests of Kielder, Redesdale and Wark (all in Northumberland), Kershope (in Cumberland) and Newcastleton and Wauchope (both in Scotland) together form the largest state forest in Britain, a total area of 280 square miles, enclosing about 180 square miles of growing trees. Planting began here in 1926, partly to counterbalance the disastrous slump which had hit the industrial district of Tyneside and the neighbouring coalfield. The greater part of the region (but excluding most of Wark Forest) is contained in the Border Forest Park, established in 1955 and extending 30 miles from north to south by 27 miles in the other direction.

Much of the country included in the Forest area was once covered with a growth of oak, birch and alder. The oak had completely disappeared; much of it was felled as agriculture spread up North Tynedale from the lower reaches, while some of the timber was taken by the Scots on predatory raids. The other species had thinned out appreciably and ex-isted mainly along the burn sides. Natural regeneration of the woodland was prevented by the development of sheep farming and its attendant burnings of the moor grasses assist the poor hill grazing. The Forestry Commission can therefore claim to have put back something that was there before, though in rather a different form.

But to those of us who had grown familiar with the upper reaches of North Tynedale as a terrain of wild, bare, breezy moorland, afforestation has changed the face of the landscape to a considerable extent, and we may have taken exception to seeing much of it submerged beneath a dense growth of conifers. Our reactions are perhaps largely based on habit; for instance, none of us who objected to the ruin of Hawes Water in the Lake District by turning it into a reservoir before the Second World War can possibly be old enough to have known the shape of Thirlmere before its similar conversion, and accept without demur its present form. In time, no doubt, we shall accept the change of scene in North Tynedale, and to the younger generation of course the problem does not present itself.

The young trees, mostly spruces, but with an intermingling of pines and larches, are planted 5 feet apart along the furrows, long slices of turf, making an average of about 1,750 trees per acre, though the trees are thinned out after about 20 years growth. These thinnings are used for making paper pulp, chipboard or hardboard and fencing; the larger timber is sawn up mainly for building and making packages. The planting of the forests has resulted in some changes in the flora and fauna of the region. Among the animals the roe deer, the red squirrel and (more rarely) the pine marten may be seen, while pheasants and other woodland birds have now made themselves at home here. The forests are perhaps at their most attractive in spring, when new leaves are appearing on the larches, and in the autumn, when they are changing colour.

The Forestry Commission has changed not only the appearance but the fundamental economy of the greater part of this section of the Border, and the scale of the development may be measured by the fact that in the whole area several new villages have been built or planned to house the several hundreds of workers employed in the forest. The main villages are at Stonehaugh (mentioned above), at Kielder on the North Tyne and at Byrness in Redesdale (Chapter 4), while there are smaller groups of houses near Bonchester Bridge, in Wauchope Forest, and at Kershopefoot in Liddesdale (Chapter 13). Designed specifically for their purpose by Thomas Sharp, these villages are intended to provide more than just houses for the forest workers. Each village is planned to be the focal point in the life of its immediate neighbourhood, and in consequence each has (or is planned to have) its own church, inn, shops and village hall. The new houses are white-fronted and entirely different in style from the existing rather dour grey houses in the dales.

The forest roads and tracks are accessible to walkers at most times, but cars are allowed only on the public roads (thank goodness). In the forests are numerous picnic places, waymarked walks and hides for bird-watching, and information centres have been opened at Kielder Castle and Byrness. Camping grounds have been set aside at Lewisburn (with a caravan site, too) and Byrness (both administered by the Camping Club).

At the time of writing, a new man-made lake, the Kielder Reservoir, is being created in the upper part of North Tynedale. The dam, to be 170 feet high and 3,750 feet long, is being built at Yarrow, about a mile above Falstone. The area of the reservoir, to be the largest in Britain, will be 2,800 acres and the capacity about 44,200 million gallons. When it is completed, by about 1980, facilities will be provided for sailing and other sporting activities.

Between Falstone and Plashetts, on the north side of the valley, a small 'land sale' colliery still exists, though the colliery village has long since been deserted. It is known to have been working before 1812; at first it provided fuel for lime-burning the pastures, but soon the coal was being transported into Scotland, travelling by an old drove road that starts from Mounces, on the river below Plashetts, goes up the Akenshaw Burn to cross the Border at Bloody Bush (where some skirmish must have taken place) and descends thence to Dinlabyre in Liddesdale (Chapter 13). Bridges bear the date 1828 and on the Border line is a toll stone giving distances along the road and the charges levied on the drovers. The period of greatest output from the colliery seems to have been about 1870, though probably the coal was sent by the North British Railway after it penetrated the valley in 1862.

The North Tyne decreases in breadth as the outlet of each tributary burn is passed. Many of these waters, the Chirdon Burn (already mentioned), the Whickhope Burn (above Yarrow), the Lewis Burn and the Kielder Burn, are as fine in their way as any in the Border. Near the confluence of the Lewis Burn, in a cottage probably of the seventeenth century or earlier, is a small museum illustrating the natural and social history of the region. The road, which has kept to the south side of the river, passes the Kielder Viaduct, a 'skew' bridge which carried the railway over the North Tyne until 1958, and farther on are the white houses, built in 1952, of the Forestry Commission village of Kielder.

Kielder Castle, which stands on a plateau above the other bank of the river, has nothing medieval about it. A shooting lodge built in 1775 for the Duke of Northumberland, it is now a recreation and information centre, with a forestry exhibition, a workingmen's club (perhaps the most palatially housed in Britain) and a refreshment room. A new forest drive, 12 miles long and open to cars, leads through woodland and up over the moors before descending to Byrness in Redesdale. It starts up the west bank of the Kielder Burn and reaches a height of 1481 feet (the highest road summit in the Border) at Blakehope Nick, a moorland saddle from which a wild and lonely prospect spreads all around, best appreciated at sundown, when all the other cars have gone home. Walkers and horse-riders may continue up the Kielder Burn and its tributary the White Kielder, then continue over the watershed at Girdle Fell (1746 feet) and down north of the fall of Chattlehope Spout to the Catcleugh Reservoir.

Above Kielder the North Tyne is joined by the Bells Burn, in an attractive little glen and forming the Border for part of its course. On the high ground above the river here once stood the village of Bells, or Bells Kirk. Mentioned as far back as 1326 as 'within the lordship of Tynedale', it was later one of the meeting places of the Lords Wardens of the Marches. By 1551 it was 'within the bounds of Liddesdale', thus showing that the actual Border line was never rigidly adhered to. The 'kirk' was probably an outpost of the priory of Canonbie, on the Esk. In 1715 Bells was described as a 'mean village ... where are the ruins of an old chapel', but both village and chapel have disappeared.

The road reaches the Border and the head of the North Tyne beyond the farm of Deadwater, well named, as the source of the river in the marshy ground is difficult to locate. We are here on the edge of the forest and the surrounding landscape shows us what the moorlands bounding North Tynedale were like before they were afforested. This is still a country of exhilarating spaciousness and freedom:

> *On Kielder side the wind blaws wide,*
> *There sounds nae hunting horn*
> *That rings sae sweet as the winds that beat*
> *Round banks where Tyne is born,*

as Swinburne sang in *A Jacobite's Exile*, the most moving of his Northumbrian poems.

The Deadwater Burn comes down to join the North Tyne from the side of Peel Fell (1975 feet), a 'stern and dark-hued hill', up the lower slopes of which the forest now climbs. The summit, the highest point on the Border range south of the Coquet, is remarkable for the extent of its view. To the north-east is the great bulk of Cheviot, to the north and north-west are the Southern Uplands of Scotland (the Lammermuirs, the Moorfoots and Ettrick Forest), westward are Criffel and the hills of Galloway, and south-west are the mountains of the Lake District, while between these groups a flash of shimmering water denotes the Solway

Firth. To the south are the high Pennines, culminating in Cross Fell; to the east, across a great expanse of Northumberland, the North Sea is said to be visible on a clear day. If this be so, Peel Fell must be one of the few places in England from which the sea can be seen on both sides. The Kielder Stone, a huge detached outcrop of the fell-sandstone up to 26 feet high, on the Border line, a mile east of Peel Fell, is reputed to have been used as a Border 'post office', where letters were left by messengers of one country until it was safe to collect them from the other.

From Deadwater started an old road known as the Wheel Causey or Causeway, often attributed to the Romans, though there is no evidence that they ever came this way. The causeway crossed the Peel Burn and went on over Wheelrig Head (1465 feet) to the Rule Water. In medieval times it was the main road to Roxburgh, then the most important town in Scotland, and in 1296 Edward I travelled by this route on his entry into Scotland, spending a night at a chapel known as the Wheel Kirk, now vanished. The southern part of the road has been superseded by a more recent track through Peel Farm, and on the northern side it now runs through Wauchope Forest. Another old route across the Border, referred to in 1543 as the Carter Road, ran from Kielder Head over the peaty wastes of Knox Knowe (1636 feet; formerly Knock's), the south-west shoulder of Carter Fell, and down to Southdean, on the Jed Water (Chapter 13).

Over the watershed, the road from North Tynedale, leaving the forest, drops down below Thorlieshope into Liddesdale.

CHAPTER FOUR

From Corbridge to Redesdale

The road from Hexham (Chapter 3) to Corbridge and Newcastle, starting on the south side of the broad and beautifully-wooded valley of the Tyne, crosses a fine reach of the river by a bridge of 1674, the only one over the river to withstand a tremendous flood in 1771. Corbridge, now a large village, on the high north bank, succeeded Bamburgh as the capital of Northumbria in the 8th century. Later, like Hexham, it suffered from the incursions of the Scots; within 40 years it was burned by Wallace, Bruce and David II, and of its four old churches only one now stands. This was mostly rebuilt in the Early English style in the thirteenth century, incorporating a twelfth-century south doorway, as well as the tower of an early Saxon church, of the 8th century, one of the earliest surviving examples of ecclesiastical building in the Border. The lower part of the tower previously formed a porch, while the tower arch has been transferred in its entirety from a Roman gateway at *Corstopitum*.

At the edge of the churchyard is an early fourteenth-century pele tower (likewise built of Roman stones) that originally formed a refuge for the priest (it is now an information centre). The Angel Inn, facing the bridge, is partly of the seventeenth century; of the two charming houses at the entrance to the village from the direction of Newcastle, one incorporates an old pele tower. Border villages are often characterised by a rugged solidity and an atmosphere of wary vigilance, but Corbridge appears unusually peaceful and inviting. It has a broad market place, and pleasant gardens in the wide main street and dropping towards the river.

The quiet road returning towards Hexham on the north side of the Tyne passes the entrance to *Corstopitum* (the stress is on the second

syllable), where the remains of a complete Roman town are still in process
of excavation. A fort was established on this site some time after A.D. 78
by Agricola, who had built the Stanegate (Chapter 2) through the Tyne
Gap from Carlisle, or possibly by his successor. Agricola had also built the
road from York to the Tyne now called Dere Street, and he subsequently
pushed this forward across Redesdale and up over the Border. After about
123 the garrison of *Corstopitum* was transferred to the new cavalry fort of
Onnum, on Hadrian's Wall (Chapter 2), but the fort was re-occupied by
139, during the governorship of Lollius Urbicus, and became the supply
depôt for the armies marching northward along Dere Street into what is
now Scotland. The existing structures at *Corstopitum* belong mainly to the
early part of the 3rd century, after the period of the Emperor Severus, by
which time the town had developed into a market centre and an important military base for provisioning the defences of the Wall. They were
altered again, after 296, during the reign of Constantius Chlorus, and yet
again after 367, when Hadrian's Wall fell to a combined attack of the
Picts, the Scots and the Saxons. *Corstopitum* ceased to function as a
military base late in the 4th century, shortly before the wholesale
withdrawal of the Roman forces from Britain.

Corstopitum stands on a low plateau bounded on one side by the stony
Tyne and on another by the little Cor Burn, near the mouth of which may
be seen, when the water is low, fragments of the bridge that brought the
road from York over the river. The remains of buildings now exposed in
the town include two long and narrow granaries of the orthodox Roman
type, with their massive buttresses, stone-flagged floors with an extensive
ventilation system beneath, and the bases of columns of a raised loading
platform at the front. To the east of these are remains of an elaborate
fountain, with part of its feed-channel. A large unfinished building, farther
east, enclosing a square courtyard, may have been intended as a legionary
headquarters (Severus is thought to have considered establishing one
here), but became a great storehouse (one of the largest Roman buildings
in Britain). On the other side of the main street (part of the Stanegate) are
two remarkable compounds for making weapons and equipment, complete with their own offices and workshops; and on either side of these
are the ruins of buildings thought to have been used as temples. In the interesting museum are coins and pottery, some ingeniously reconstructed
inscriptions and a sculptured fountain-head known as the 'Corbridge lion'.

In 1955 a bath-house of the Agricolan period was discovered near Beaufront Red House, three-quarters of a mile west of *Corstopitum*. This posed a problem for the archaeologists, as it seemed too early and too far away to have served the fort. The building of a new by-pass for Hexham and Corbridge, north of the Tyne, gave an opportunity for excavation in 1974 just to the west of the bath-house. This revealed signs of a turf and timber fort, with traces of buildings (probably workshops and barrack blocks), dating from about A.D. 70 but dismantled before the end of the 1st century, by which time the Romans had moved their military base to a new site at *Corstopitum*. This they did probably because the original fort stood on a terrace above the Tyne and could only have been enlarged by extending it on to the flood plain of the river. Beaufront Castle (pronounced 'Bo-'), standing prominently on a hill overlooking the site and the Tyne, is a Gothic house built in 1837–41 by John Dobson of Newcastle.

Dere Street, leaving *Corstopitum* on the north, can be seen running through the fields as a bank or 'agger'. It joins the main road from Corbridge to Redesdale and climbs steeply out of the Tyne valley to reach Stagshawbank, where it passed through Hadrian's Wall by the Portgate. The road was still used, centuries after the Roman withdrawal, as one of the main drove roads to Scotland, and when the Military Road was constructed in the eighteenth century this became an important cross-roads. Stagshawbank was long the scene of a famous fair, held as many as six times a year, from May to October. 'It is tempting to conjecture', wrote R. G. Collingwood in the first volume of *The Oxford History of England*, 'that Stagshawbank Fair is the lineal successor of the market where ... traders sold goods brought past the custom house at Portgate.'

Beyond the Portgate the modern road, following the Roman road, continues north over undulating, sparsely-inhabited country, passing near the farm of Beukley, high on a ridge, where another Roman road, called the Devil's Causeway, goes off to the north-east, taking an almost direct course across Northumberland towards Berwick. The toll-house beside the main road is one of the few survivals of the turnpike era.

From Beukley the course of Dere Street can be seen, going straight on northwards across the high, bleak uplands. It crosses the road from Hexham to Rothbury, along which, to the left, is the village of Chollerton, above the east bank of the North Tyne. The church, much rebuilt in about

1769, has a south arcade of about 1150 built of Roman monolithic columns, brought probably from Chesters, and a Roman altar that has been scooped out at the top for use as a font. At the churchyard gate is a rare stable, possibly of the eighteenth century, where churchgoers who had to come from a distance could leave their horses.

Approaching the valley of the Swin Burn, the modern road makes a divergence to the east from Dere Street, to the west of which is the secluded hamlet of Great Swinburne. The seventeenth- to eighteenth-century house of Swinburne Castle, like its medieval predecessor, is now unhappily in ruins. This was the ancestral home of the Swinburnes, an old Northumbrian family, though in the seventeenth-century they moved to Capheaton Hall, near the Newcastle-Otterburn road.

In the park of Swinburne Castle are reminders of prehistoric times, some distinctive lynchets, or cultivation terraces, several burial mounds (in one of which was found a Bronze Age jet necklace) and a tall monolith, 11 feet high, the finest standing stone in the Border. Many prehistoric enclosures are to be seen in the country around Swinburne, the best perhaps those to the east of Dere Street, near the lane to the Swinburne limestone quarries. About a mile north of these is the pele tower of Little Swinburne, built some time after 1415; and on top of a rocky outcrop a mile farther on (with a wide view towards Hadrian's Wall and the Pennines) is the small and almost solitary church of Thockrington. The church is basically Norman, but the original rounded end, or apse, was replaced by a straight east end in the thirteenth century. The church has heavy buttresses and a square bell-cote, and the chancel has a remarkable tunnel vault with the window arches cut into it, probably as late as the seventeenth century, of the type to be seen only at Bellingham and elsewhere in the Border counties. Lord Beveridge, who has been called the 'father of the Welfare State', lived at Carrycoats Hall, away to the west, and was buried in the churchyard here in 1963.

The modern road, rejoining Dere Street, skirts the sombre, wood-enclosed Colt Crag Reservoir, which supplies Newcastle. The small farm of Waterfalls, to the north of the solitary Tone Inn, was the meeting place of the Jacobite rebels, under the Earl of Derwentwater, in 1715. A moorland road farther on leads east across country towards Kirkwhelpington, near the Newcastle-Otterburn road, passing the lonely lakes of Sweethope Loughs. The fell-sandstone outcrops of the Great

Wanney Crags, to the north, have long been a favourite rock-climbing ground.

Near the farm of Fourlaws, the main road takes a considerable bend to the east of Dere Street, and on the left, just before this point, are the ramparts of a Roman marching camp, almost square in plan, one of many to be seen between here and the Border. The main road takes an easier course through the hamlet of Ridsdale, while the Roman road, after crossing Chesterhope Common, plunges straight down into the valley of the Rede. To the west are the spoil heaps of ironstone mining. Iron is said to have been worked here in Roman times and in the last century the Ridsdale Ironworks supplied material for Lord Armstrong's foundry at Elswick, on the Tyne above Newcastle, established in 1847. Remains of kilns and furnaces can be seen and the engine house resembles a medieval tower-house.

Dere Street crosses the Rede north of the fort of Risingham, the Roman *Habitancum*, the first of the outpost forts beyond Hadrian's Wall. The meagre visible remains, on private land and much overgrown, stand on a low plateau overlooking the river and are approached by a farm road from West Woodburn. The fort, founded during the time of Severus, was remodelled after 297 (when the west gate was inserted and Dere Street taken past on that side, perhaps because the river had changed course) and it was occupied until not later than 367. The modern road crosses the Rede at the small village of West Woodburn, then climbs from the river to pick up the line of Dere Street again and skirts the broad expanse of Corsenside Common. Beside a road crossing the common to Hareshaw Head, near a prehistoric burial-mound, a Roman milestone has been re-erected, and from this point the main road forms the boundary of the National Park as far as Elishaw.

On the right is the small and isolated church of Corsenside, of Norman origin, but altered in the eighteenth century, when new windows were inserted. There seems never to have been a village at Corsenside, any more than at Thockrington, and these lonely churches were presumably built to serve the scattered farmsteads. Reaching a road from Bellingham, we leave the Roman road, which goes on to Elishaw, passing the farm of Troughend, on the site of the hall of Percy Reed, whose death was the subject of a sorrowful ballad, and the earthworks of two rectangular marching camps, at Dargues and Blakehope. These camps were intended for temporary occupation while the Romans were pushing forward from Hadrian's Wall to establish themselves in what is now the Border Country.

We cross the broad, green strath of the Rede to Otterburn Mill, which has been making tweeds and woollen goods for over 150 years, the power being provided by water channelled off the river. Otterburn is an unremarkable village on the eternally busy main road between Newcastle and Edinburgh by way of Jedburgh, but it is delightfully situated above the strath where the river turns southward on its way towards the North Tyne. We turn first towards Newcastle, but in less than a mile branch left towards Elsdon, with Colwell Hill, topped by the double ramparts of an Iron Age hill-fort, to the left, and the moory ridges of the Ottercops away to the right, beyond the Elsdon Burn.

Elsdon, the historic capital of the liberty of Redesdale, conveys the atmosphere of being one of the remotest villages in the Border, but it was formerly an important market centre, at the junction of several drove roads. It has eighteenth-century and other old houses, scattered round a very large green that was once busy with sheep and cattle and their dealers. On the green is the fourteenth-century church (the centre of a vast parish stretching away to the Border line), with unusual half-barrel vaulted ceilings, perhaps of the seventeenth century, in the aisles of the nave and transepts. When the church was undergoing restoration in the last century over 1,000 skulls were discovered, conjectured to be those of English soldiers who fell at the Battle of Otterburn. In the churchyard is the tombstone of Thomas Wilson, who died in 1778, 'officer for the duty of salt', reminding us that Elsdon was on one of the 'Salters' Roads' to Scotland. Above the green stands the embattled rectory, or priest's house, the finest example of this kind of fortification in the Border. Built in about 1400 by the Umfraville family, it has served its present purpose from the outset.

On the north of the village, near the beginning of the lonely road which crosses to the valley of the Coquet, for Rothbury (Chapter 5), are the so-called Mote Hills, perhaps formed in the first place by the accumulation of detritus thrown down by the rushing burn, but adapted as part of a Norman motte-and-bailey castle by Robert de Umfraville early in the twelfth century, on being granted the lordship of Redesdale. The castle was abandoned after 1157, when Henry II recovered the earldom of Northumberland from the Scots and transferred the capital of the liberty to Harbottle, in Coquetdale, and only the earthworks now remain.

From Otterburn the Jedburgh road goes up the open Redesdale, which has an atmosphere of barren and spacious wildness that is the epitome of 'all the wild Border'. Its rolling, prairie-like uplands, stretching out in every direction, are covered with coarse grasses (locally called 'bents') intermixed with rushes, whose whiteness as they decay in the autumn gives the landscape an even more desolate appearance. Though traversed by one of the main roads from Newcastle to Edinburgh and encroached on by the large plantations of the Forestry Commission, it yet conveys the impression of great spaciousness and freedom.

It may be this sense of spaciousness, if not loneliness, that accounts for Redesdale's long-standing reputation, in former times, for lawless and primitive living surpassing that of any other valley on either side of the Border; the forays of the Scots were not more feared in the neighbouring valleys than those of the Redesdale men. The isolation of their windswept moors no doubt inculcated a dislike of rule and order and a freedom from restraint in the dalesmen; they acknowledged no law and feared no-one except their own neighbours, and their main occupations were robbing and fighting with each other. The laws of the Marches, the reports of Royal Commissions, the chronicles and records are full of accounts of raids and forays, feuds and incursions, and of the vain efforts of the Government and the Wardens of the Marches to impose some restraint on the Redesdale men. Long after the rest of the country had settled down under the peaceful and profitable rule of the Tudors, lawlessness continued in the dale.

The road up Redesdale passes near Percy's Cross, of which the lower part is probably medieval, though the cross (which has no head) seems to have been moved here in about 1777. It was long thought to mark the site of the Battle of Otterburn, fought in 1388, probably on the slopes to the north, and sung by the English in the ballad of *Chevy Chase* and by the Scots in the *Battle of Otterbourne*. Otterburn was not one of the decisive battles of history, but it surpasses the typical Border foray in that it was one of the most desperately fought and brought to a climax the long and bitter hatred between two of the great houses of England and Scotland. 'I never heard the olde song of Percy and Douglas', wrote the Elizabethan Sir Philip Sidney in his *Apologie for Poetrie*, 'that I found not my heart mooved more then with a Trumpet and yet is it sung but by some blind crowder, with no rougher voice than rude style.' The story is also recounted in great detail, and with greater accuracy than in the ballads, in the *Chronicles* of Sir John Froissart, who gathered his information from the participants. The young Earl of Douglas was killed, but the fiery Hotspur (whom we shall meet again at Alnwick) and his brother, Sir Ralph Percy, were captured and the skirmish ended in the rout of the English.

The Jedburgh road is joined by the road from Corbridge at the farm of Elishaw, on the boundary of the National Park. This locality was once a gathering place of drovers, carriers and the like. 'Many a scene of revelry and carousal used to be witnessed here', said W. W. Tomlinson, in his *Comprehensive Guide to Northumberland*, 'for Elishaw was a famous resort of faws, tinkers, and pedlars, and here they held their rustic races and merry gatherings.' Our road crosses the line of Dere Street as it passes through a Roman marching camp and before reaching the scattered hamlet of Horsley. The church here, built in 1844, has a Roman altar from Featherwood in the porch. Evistones, on the other side of the Rede, is now the centre of the Redesdale Experimental Husbandry Farm, established in 1967 by the National Agricultural Advisory Service and comprising some 2,300 acres of varied farmland extending up to the moors. On the slopes to the west of the farm are the remains of a medieval settlement, still occupied in 1604, when all the tenants bore the name of Fletcher.

From the hamlet of Rochester (pronounced 'Ro-'), a lane ascends to High Rochester, where the farmstead is enclosed by the scanty remains of the Roman fort of *Bremenium*, which stood on Dere Street just above the place where the road forded the Sills Burn on its way towards the heights of the Border. The fort, founded by Agricola, was rebuilt in about 139 by Lollius Urbicus and altered during the reigns of Severus and Constantius Chlorus. The west gateway has endured and part of the outer wall can be traced.

The main road skirts the southern boundary of the Redesdale Artillery Range, a vast military training ground which began as a comparatively circumscribed area near Rochester, but was enlarged during the Second World War to take in an enormous tract of country, some 70 square miles in extent, stretching almost from Otterburn as far north as Windy

Gyle on the Border and including the whole of the upper reaches of the Coquet and the grand moorland country on either side of it. The range is officially closed to the public when firing is in progress, and the drivers of private cars having no specific business in the area may find themselves stopped at the boundaries. Yet all this huge artillery range is inside the Northumberland National Park!

A road made by the army follows the line of Dere Street northward over empty moorland between the Sills Burn and the enormous cairn of stones (originally a Neolithic burial mound) on Bellshiel Law (1068 feet). Beyond the solitary farm of Featherwood the new road passes two huge marching camps, their ditches defined by a growth of rushes, and two large stones with holes in them called the Middle and Outer Golden Pots. These were probably the bases of boundary crosses, though they may have marked the line of a drove road, known in medieval times as Gammel's Path, probably from the Danish 'gamel', meaning old. The drove road followed the Roman road down to the camps at Chew Green, at the head of the Coquet (Chapter 5).

At Woolaw and Birdhope, on the other side of the Rede from the army camp, are remains of native settlements of the Roman period that were occupied again in the Middle Ages. The Jedburgh road enters the northern part of Redesdale Forest, a section of the Border Forest Park (Chapter 3), and runs between serried ranks of conifers. The Pennine Way comes down on the south through the forest to Blakehopeburnhaugh farm, then ascends beside the river to the hamlet of Byrness, from which it climbs northward out of the dale and the forest to Byrness Hill (1358 feet), on the way to the Border and the Chew Green camps.

At Byrness, which has a small church of 1786 (altered in 1884) and the last hotel in England, the first sheepdog trial in England was held, in 1876. This is the terminal point of the forest drive which leads over from Kielder Castle, in North Tynedale (Chapter 3), and half a mile farther on are the white houses of the Forestry Commission village. The road leaves the forest and skirts the Catcleugh Reservoir (pronounced '-cluf') of the Newcastle and Gateshead waterworks, constructed in 1905 and charmingly encompassed by trees. The steep, green hills begin to encroach on the river, and the road ascends more sharply. The forest we have left, though out of character with the surrounding moorland, does at least serve to accentuate the extreme desolation of these head reaches of the Rede.

The road reaches the Border at Carter Bar (1370 feet), on the site of the medieval crossing known as the Redeswire, referred to in John Barbour's epic poem, *The Brus*, written about 1376. This was one of the meeting places of the Wardens of the Middle Marches, and the site of the 'Raid of the Reidswire' in 1575, sung in the last Border ballad. The bluff rising to the west of the pass and facing into Scotland is Catcleuch Shin (the 'ch' is hard, as in 'loch') and a comparison of the pronounciation of this with Catcleugh illustrates the difference in speech between the two sides of the Border. Each adopts the form most suitable to its particular intonation.

From Carter Bar we have a splendid view along the Border and into Scotland. The Cheviots, the Lammermuirs, the Eildon Hills and the heights of Ettrick Forest are all in view, and the road is seen zigzagging down towards Jedburgh (Chapter 13). This exhilarating crossing of the Border is best enjoyed in that long twilight of a summer evening, when the cars have mostly gone home, the pungent scents of the moorland grasses fill the air, the grouse rise hurriedly from heathery clumps, shouting their guttural 'go-back, go-back,' and the hills begin to assume a huge, dark and mysterious outline.

CHAPTER FIVE

Coquetdale and the Vale of Whittingham

The Coquet (pronounced 'Kó-ket') is the most delightful and best loved river between the Tyne and the Tweed, and is an especial favourite with anglers, as it is probably the richest water in the Border for trout and salmon may also be caught. The river rises right on the boundary of England and Scotland, near the Roman forts at Chew Green, and pursues a long, meandering course, at first through a deep and tortuous valley among the steep hills, grass and bracken covered, which form the southern edge of the Cheviots, where it hurtles along with the impetuosity of a mountain stream. Leaving the hills, it winds across an open, pastoral vale, over a pebble-strewn bed among green haughs or meadows; then cuts a restricted passage through the fell-sandstone range of Rothbury Forest; and finally, threads a narrow glen, between green banks and hanging woods, on its journey to reach the sea beyond Warkworth (Chapter 8).

The road ascending the Coquet from Weldon Bridge, on the New-castle-Wooler road, and passing near the exquisite late-twelfth-century church of Brinkburn Priory, skirts the splendid estate of Cragside, laid out for the first Lord Armstrong, the famous engineer and inventor, a great tract of rich woodland, where conifers, though predominating, are pleasingly mixed with deciduous trees, and with some small but charming lakes. Higher up, the trees give place to moorland with a thick growth of heather. The grounds, open to the public, are at their best in June, when the many clumps of rhododendrons display a wealth of colour. The rambling house, though a curious mingling of styles, tones well with its wooded surroundings. Designed in 1870 by R. Norman Shaw, it can be compared with the same architect's house at Chesters, near Hadrian's Wall, in quite a different setting.

Near the west end of the ravine is the delightfully placed small town of Rothbury, the acknowledged capital of Coquetdale. Long an important market centre, especially for the sale of sheep, it has become a favourite summer resort, as witnessed by the many villas that have sprung up around it. This popularity Rothbury owes to its unrivalled situation, enjoying the untainted air of the surrounding moorlands, yet from its position low in the valley sheltered from the more vigorous winds. The older part of the town consists mainly of a single wide street of pleasant stone houses, mounting an irregular slope on each side of a green sheltered by sycamores.

What is now open, breezy moorland stretching from the Simonside Hills to the Vale of Whittingham was in primeval times a large expanse of forest, and Rothbury first existed as a clearance in this. Vestiges of Iron Age settlement may be seen in the double rampart and ditch of a fort on the slope to the west of the town. After the Norman Conquest, the manor of Rothbury remained a possession of the Crown for nearly a century and a half, but in 1205 it was given to Robert FitzRoger of Warkworth by King John, who also granted the first market charter. Later Rothbury passed to the Percys of Alnwick, who have held it ever since. The town suffered more than most places in the Middle Ages from the scourge of indiscriminate plundering, raiders coming not only from across the Border but also from neighbouring valleys such as Redesdale. The people of Rothbury themselves, however, appear not to have been entirely faultless; they were described as 'amongst the wildest and most uncivilised in the county. For fighting, gaming and drinking they had a worse reputation than the inhabitants of Tynedale and Redesdale.'

The parish church at Rothbury was largely rebuilt in 1850 and does not exhibit anything of particular interest, except for the font, which has a bowl dated 1664 supported by a pedestal which was discovered during the rebuilding. This is part of the shaft of a finely carved Northumbrian cross (the head is in the Museum of Antiquities in Newcastle University), dated to about A.D. 800 and therefore one of the oldest examples of Christian carving in Britain. The bridge over the Coquet below the church incorporates three arches of a medieval bridge built probably in the fifteenth century. Whatever aesthetic value it may have had, however, was destroyed when it was widened by the Northumberland County Council and given an ugly new parapet. (The County Council seems to be particularly unimaginative on the subject of bridges, frequently putting up hideous iron structures where the landscape cries out for stone bridges.)

The road to the right beyond the bridge ascends to the hamlet of Whitton, which has a fortified rectory similar to those at Elsdon and Corbridge, built in the fourteenth century by one of the powerful Umfraville family (and now a children's home). The road continues westward, entering the National Park and climbing to the farmsteads of Great Tosson, with the remnants of a pele, one of a chain of towers that once extended along the length of Coquetdale.

Great Tosson lies at the northern foot of the striking fell-sandstone range of the Simonside Hills, well seen from Rothbury. Though attaining no very great elevation (Tosson Hill, the highest point, is only 1444 feet) the range is conspicuous on three counts: its isolated position, thrust out from the main body of the Border hills, whereby it can be seen from many places in Northumberland; its craggy tops, giving it a boldness of outline generally lacking among the more rounded summits of the neighbouring Cheviot Hills; and its great wealth of heather, again in marked contrast to the grassy Cheviots.

The most striking summit and the one most worth ascending is that which gives its name to the whole range. The route to Simonside (1409 feet) ascends through a new forest, from which an easy climb reaches the saddle between Raven's Heugh (1385 feet) and the tumbled crags of the name peak, from the top of which an exceptionally wide view is unfolded. To the north-west, beyond Coquetdale, stretches a great panorama of the Cheviot Hills, embracing all the highest summits; southward one looks over a vast expanse of barren moorish country (now partly encroached on by Harwood Forest), and in this direction the distant Pennines can be seen when the weather is clear. 'Heugh' (pronounced 'heuff') means a crag, and the rock faces of Raven's Heugh, like those of Simonside, are now a favourite climbing ground. Another is Selby's Cove, to the south of Simonside near the head of the Forest Burn. But this is lonely country, lying well above the limits of the farms, and, except in high summer, very few people are to be met with.

The most interesting way back to Rothbury from Simonside is to walk eastward over Dove Crag (1295 feet) and descend towards Garleigh

Moor. On a prominent spur of the range is the Iron Age hill-fort of Lordenshaws, one of the largest and finest in the Border, with three distinct ramparts and ditches, enclosing some particularly well-preserved hut-circles of a Romano-British settlement. In the neighbourhood are several Bronze Age burial mounds and some of those mysterious rock-sculptures that still baffle the archaeologist. These usually consist of a shallow 'cup' carved on the rock, surrounded by one or more concentric rings, though others have no rings; sometimes the cup has a small channel leading out of it, and occasionally other figures, such as rectangles, are introduced. They are most frequently, though not invariably, found on exposed rocks on high places, and they are conjectured to have had some connection either with the religion or with the burial rites of their prehistoric designers.

The shortest route from Rothbury to Upper Coquetdale goes through Thropton, north of the river. More interesting is the quiet lane from Whitton running below Great Tosson and the northern escarpment of the Simonsides, with a fine view across the pastoral dale to the Cheviots. The roads come together below the Iron Age promontory fort of Witchy Neuk, said to have been one of the landing places of Meg o' Meldon, a local witch. It faces the opposite hill-fort of Harehaugh across the mouth of the Grasslees Burn, up which the road to Elsdon (Chapter 4) runs through Billsmoor Park, a delightful region of heather and bracken, birch and alder, where the roe-deer may sometimes be seen.

A road continues up the Coquet to Holystone, a secluded hamlet of engaging irregularity, its gardens gay with flowers in summer. From the little Salmon Inn a path leads to the so-called Lady's Well, a clear spring hidden in a copse, which stood beside a Roman road from High Rochester (Chapter 4) to join the Devil's Causeway and may itself be Roman in origin. Here the missionary Paulinus is supposed to have baptized 3,000 Northumbrians at Easter, A.D. 627, though in fact there is no record of his having been in this district. On Holystone Common, to the south, is a group of Bronze Age burial mounds called the Five Barrows.

The ruins of Harbottle Castle are seen, on a green mound rising above the trees, before the road descends to the village, one of the most attractive in Coquetdale, with cottages of grey-brown sandstone hemmed in by the castle mound on one side and by a ridge of crag-topped moorlands on the other. The first castle here, probably taking advantage of a natural knoll, as at Elsdon, was built by Robert de Umfraville, to whom William the Conqueror had granted the wide and wild domain of Redesdale, which at that time included all the country between that valley and the Coquet. The castle whose crumbling remains are now to be seen was built by Henry II on the return of Northumberland from under Scottish jurisdiction. It followed the pattern of the previous stronghold, consisting of outer and inner baileys, raised on the semicircular knoll, with the keep on its motte at the corner of the inner bailey. Both baileys were enclosed by a curtain wall and surrounded by a ditch, except where the steep slope to the Coquet made this unnecessary.

Not long after its completion the castle was captured by William the Lion of Scotland, but after his defeat outside Alnwick it reverted to the Umfravilles, who remained until 1415. In 1515, Margaret Tudor, who had married Archibald Douglas, Earl of Angus, after the death of her first husband, James IV, at Flodden (Chapter 10), gave birth here to a daughter who became the grandmother of James I of England. But Harbottle was too near the Border for safety, and immediately after her confinement she was removed to Cartington Castle (on the edge of the moors north of Rothbury) and thence to Morpeth. By 1541 Harbottle Castle was reported as being in 'great decay', and though its repair was several times suggested, as much to 'distress the thieves of Redesdale' as to check the inroads of the Scots, it remained a ruin.

Harbottle, like Elsdon, had a market in medieval times, and in 1279 Gilbert de Umfraville was claiming that his ancestors had levied tolls at these markets 'from time immemorial', but they took the 'crossing tax' at Elishaw in Redesdale from Scotsmen only. Harbottle became the capital on the English side of the Middle March, which extended from the Hanging Stone on Cheviot, where it met the boundary of the East March, to the head of the Kershope Burn, where it coincided with that of the West March. On Harbottle Crag, west of the village, is the Drake Stone, a prominent fell-sandstone boulder about 30 feet high.

The road on from Harbottle crosses the Coquet to the church of Alwinton (once called Allenton), the chancel of which dates back to the twelfth century, though the nave was largely rebuilt in 1851. Because of the slope of the ground, the chancel stands ten steps above the nave and the altar yet another three steps higher. The small village, the highest in Coquetdale, is beautifully situated between the Coquet and its principal tributary, the Alwin, just above the point where these waters meet after emerging from their constricted valleys in the Cheviot Hills.

The Alwin, with other tributaries on the north of the Coquet, drains a large tract of hill country extending as far as the Border and known in medieval times as Kidland. From 1181 until the Dissolution of the Monasteries this remote and lonely region belonged to Newminster Abbey (on the Wansbeck above Morpeth), grants of land having been made by the Umfravilles. During the later Middle Ages the monastery found it convenient to lease the land to local shepherds, who were not only better fitted to withstand the frequent forays of the Scots, but were by no means averse to replenishing their own stocks by making reprisal raids. Kidland is still purely shepherding country today, and must remain very much as it appeared then.

The Alwin (the 'white river') is one of the least known Cheviot waters, partly because there is no road through its deep, winding dale, and partly owing to the lack of well-marked tracks leading out from its head. This is guarded by the high hills of Cushat Law (2020 feet), the fifth in height of the Cheviot Hills, and Bloodybush Edge (2001 feet), whose name is supposed to record some long-forgotten skirmish. At the foot of the southern slopes of Cushat Law are the very scanty remains of Memmerkirk, long thought to have been a chapel built by the monks of Newminster Abbey for their devotions while tending their sheep among the hills during the summer months. Excavation has shown it to have been a medieval longhouse, a type of farmstead in which the farmer's family lived at one end while the cow-byre was at the other, all under the same roof.

At the entrance to the dale is the house of Clennell, incorporating a much-modernised pele tower of 1365. A curious and interesting open-air market used to be held a little higher up the dale. Up the ridge to the west starts the green trackway of Clennell Street, skirting round a conspicuous promontory fort, with a splendid view back over the middle reach of Coquetdale to the rugged Simonside Hills. The 'Street' is not Roman, but an old drove road referred to in medieval charters as 'magnum viam de Yarnspath'. Gaining the crest of the ridge, it passes the old white shepherd's cottage of Wholehope (pronounced 'Wool-up'), now a youth hostel, before crossing the flanks of Yarnspath Law and descending to ford the Usway Burn on its way to Cocklawgate and Kirk Yetholm (Chapter 6).

Alwinton is the gateway to Upper Coquetdale, the road up which has pushed farther and farther into the hills and now extends as far as Fulhope, nearly 10 miles above Alwinton and about 2 miles from the Border at the Chew Green forts. But in just over a mile from Alwinton we reach the boundary of the Redesdale Artillery Range (Chapter 4). Access is permitted at all times to the farms in Coquetdale and the tributary valleys, but when the red flags are flying it may be dangerous to stray on to the hills and the military roads from Fulhope over to Rochester and Byrness will be closed to the public. (Information about access may be obtained by telephoning Otterburn 241.)

The road enters the ravine carved by the Coquet through the hills and drops to the river again opposite Linsheeles, which takes its name from the shepherds' huts or 'sheels' that formerly stood here (as North and South Shields took their names from the fishermen's huts that once existed at the mouth of the Tyne). Farther on, at the eighteenth-century farmstead of Shillmoor, the Coquet receives the waters of the Usway Burn (pronounced 'Yoo-zay'), said to have taken its name from Oswy, King of Northumbria in the 7th century.

Continuing up Coquetdale, the road reaches the farmstead of Barrowburn. A strong Presbyterian community flourishes in Upper Coquetdale, and though the nearest chapel of the denomination is as far away as Harbottle (the 'Protestant Dissenting Congregation of Harbottle' was established early in the eighteenth century), the minister from there holds a service periodically at Barrowburn; in the farmhouse kitchen in winter, in the little school beyond the burn in summer. The school (which also houses the post office, the only one in the dale above Alwinton) has often no more than half-a-dozen pupils, some of whom have to walk to it, summer and winter, across the hills. Before the school was opened the first master, Andrew Blyth, used to go round the farmhouses, staying a few days here, a few there, to teach the children.

A little above Barrowburn, on the other side of the Coquet, is Windyhaugh (pronounced '-half', as usual). The long single-storeyed building on the west side of the present farmhouse was the original farm, and the tiny room at the farther end formerly housed a school. The monks of Newminster had a mill at Windyhaugh, and stones from it are thought to be built into the old house. The Coquet is joined farther up by the Rowhope Burn (the 'row' is pronounced hard), at the foot of which in the eighteenth century stood an inn, kept well supplied with illicit whisky concocted in many a hidden still in deep defiles among the hills, often by Highlanders who had deserted during the Jacobite campaigns.

From the junction of the two waters starts an ancient trackway, marked on the Ordnance Survey map as 'The Street', but named on General Roy's military map of 1755 as 'Clattering Path'. It mounts westward to a ridge between the Rowhope and Carlcroft Burns, then ascends over the Black Braes (1661 feet) to the Border between Mozie Law and Windy Rig, from which it descends at length over steep-flanked hills towards Hownam, on the Kale Water (Chapter 11). A cart-road goes up the burn to the farm of Rowhope, then turns up a tributary burn past Trows farm before crossing a ridge to the upper section of the Usway Burn, where it crosses Clennell Street before reaching the farm of Uswayford (referred to again in Chapter 6).

The road up the main valley, passing several more sheep-farms, ends at Fulhope, and a cart-track thence follows the much-diminished river below the heather-clad Thirlmoor (1829 feet), one of the highest hills south of the Coquet, to the uppermost farm of Makendon. A mile beyond this are the Roman forts of Chew Green, of unknown name. Suitable and at the same time easily defensible encampment sites are not readily obtainable in the broken country of the Cheviots, and this broad spur of open moorland near the source of the Coquet must have been an obvious choice as the halting place of the Roman armies marching to the north or as the permanent quarters for patrol garrisons. The striking earthworks are those of a convoy-post (with triple ditches), a labour camp and two large marching camps, but these are difficult to visualise on the ground, as they overlap to some extent, indicating several stages of development. They stand beside the Roman road of Dere Street (Chapter 4), which descends the hillside to the south and offers a fine bird's-eye view of the earthworks. Chew Green later became one of the meeting places of the Wardens of the Middle Marches.

Dere Street, followed by the Pennine Way, climbs to the Border on the eastern shoulder of Brownhart Law (1664 feet), from the top of which we have a splendid view forward into Scotland. The old road and the new walking route, passing the site of a Roman signal station, follow the Border north to Blackhall Hill (1572 feet). Dere Street descends thence into the valley of the Kale Water (Chapter 11), but we may go on by the Pennine Way along the Border line to Windy Gyle (Chapter 6), one of the highest hills of the Cheviots.

The Cheviot Hills are bounded on their south-east side by the Vale of Whittingham (pronounced 'Whit-tin-jam'), the pastoral upper valley of the River Aln, which opens from its higher end towards the middle reach of Coquetdale. From Alwinton a quiet road runs eastward towards Whittingham, with a grand view back to the village, nestling at the foot of the hills, and of the entrance to the gorge of the Alwin. Biddlestone, which stood to the left at the foot of the steep slopes of the hills, was the home of the Selbys, a well-known Northumbrian family. The house, popularly regarded as the original of Osbaldistone Hall in *Rob Roy*, though it bore little resemblance to that described in Scott's novel, has been demolished, but the Roman Catholic chapel remains, built in the mid-nineteenth century above the vaulted basement of a pele tower. In the hill behind are quarries which provide the red grit used on many roads in Northumberland.

A road following the National Park boundary continues along the southern slopes of the Cheviots, with fine views across the vale to the serrated ridge of the Simonsides and the heather-covered moors above Rothbury. It descends to Alnham (pronounced 'Yel-nom' locally), the older part of which lies in a secluded valley under the hills. The small church is in the Transitional Norman style and has a typical Northumbrian bell-cote, but it was poorly restored in 1870. Adjacent is a well-preserved pele tower built before 1541, with the usual barrel-vaulted basement. On the other side of the lane is all that remains of Alnham Castle, a profusion of turf-covered mounds, though judging from these it must once have been quite extensive. The castle was probably demolished in 1532, when the Earl of Northumberland complained to Henry VIII of the Scots having 'brunte a town of myne called Alenam with all the corne, hay and householde stuf in the said towne and also a woman'.

On Castle Hill, nearly a mile west, is a fine example of an Iron Age hill-fort. This is passed by the Salters' Road, an ancient trackway which came into use again when salt was exported from the mouth of the Tyne to Scotland. Reaching the edge of the Cheviot Hills at Alnham, the old road winds up over the heights, passing to the west of High Knowes (1294 feet), on a spur to the south of which are prehistoric enclosures with traces of timber huts. The old trackway descends to Low Bleakhope in the Breamish Valley (Chapter 6) on its way to Windy Gyle and thence to Kirk Yetholm in the Bowmont Valley.

Roads lead east from Alnham to Whittingham, now an attractive village but once a place of some consequence, the scene of a famous fair and a posting-station on one of the principal roads to Scotland. With the close of the coaching era and the building of a new main road to the east its importance began to decline. Whittingham was one of the manors granted to Lindisfarne Priory by Ceolwulf, King of Northumbria, when he retired in 737 to the seclusion of the monastery. Of its two medieval pele towers, one still survives; it was the property of the Heron family and dates back to the fifteenth century, though it was much restored in 1845.

Whittingham is divided into two parts by the diminutive Aln. That to the south is grouped round a square enclosing a green, the other is stretched along the road leading to the church, once one of the most interesting in the Border. But it was spoiled by a disastrous 'renovation' in 1840, when the upper part of the Saxon tower was demolished in favour of the present pseudo-Gothic structure and the north arcade (one arch of which was Saxon) was replaced, merely for the sake of uniformity, by a reproduction of the thirteenth-century south arcade. The original work can still be seen in the lower part of the tower (which shows the alternating 'long and short' stones at the corners that are characteristic of Saxon work), in the west angles of the nave (also with Saxon quoining) and in the tower arch, which has a 'rugged Anglian grandeur'.

To the south of Whittingham rises the long unbroken sandstone escarpment of Thrunton Crags and Callaly Crags, its steep face masked by fine woods. Callaly Castle, below the west end of the crags, is a complex building with a complicated history. The original stronghold belonged to the Callaly family before 1161, but it passed to the Claverings (from Essex) in the late thirteenth century. The present mansion incorporates a pele tower of 1415 or earlier, added to in 1619 by Robert Trollope of Newcastle for Sir John Clavering. It was enlarged in 1707 for another John Clavering, altered in 1749 (probably by James Paine, who is known to have been employed here) and altered and added to again in the nineteenth century, especially in 1893 for the Brownes, an old Northumbrian family, who had bought the property in 1877. The house contains notable furniture, plasterwork (in the Morning Room) and Gobelins tapestry panels of 1787 (in the Victorian oak ballroom). The park, stretching up to the crags, was enclosed in 1704.

To the north of Whittingham is the pleasant village of Glanton, noted for its bird research station, founded in 1930. The study of wild birds (in which this region of the Border is particularly rich) is assisted by the more controlled observations of tame birds at the station, and from here is organised the annual record of the dawn and dusk chorus throughout the British Isles. The station stands on the slopes of Glanton Hill, the eastern extremity of a long outlying spur sent down from the Cheviot Hills.

CHAPTER SIX

The Cheviot Hills

From the head of Coquetdale, the Border line strides over the Cheviot Hills (pronounced 'Chee-veot'), a range of wild, mountainous moorlands which lie partly in Northumberland, partly in Roxburghshire, though two-thirds of their area, with most of the greatest heights, are on the English side. The name is often used, somewhat vaguely, to describe the whole range of the Border uplands, from the valley of the Till to the Cumberland boundary, but it is better restricted to the hills lying north of the River Coquet, to that part, in fact, dominated by the great massif of Cheviot itself, to which the Coquet forms a natural boundary.

Cheviot (which gives its name to the group), Hedgehope, Comb Fell, Bloodybush Edge, Windy Gyle, Cairn Hill, Auchope Cairn and The Schel (or Schil), the principal heights, are all really part of the same immense mountain, and though the River Breamish, the Harthope and College Burns and the upper feeders of the Bowmont Water have all carved deep ravines in the sides of this, it is possible to walk from one to another of the tops without any great loss of height. The Coquet, however, rises some distance away from the main massif and pursues a course not related to it, and to the south of the river the character of the country changes, being of a more open, gently rolling and rather prairie-like nature, in marked contrast to the green, rounded hills and narrow, steep-sided valleys of the true Cheviot country.

The Cheviots are essentially quiet and peaceful hills. They have not, except in a few places, that highly dramatic quality that one inevitably associates with the Lake District or the wilder parts of the Scottish Highlands. Perhaps, because of this absence of some of the grander aspects of hill scenery, it may be a feeling of loneliness rather than of ex-hilaration that impresses itself on anyone who wanders over the hills for the first time. But as one learns about the absorbing historical background which they share with the rest of the Border, and sees a little into the life of the hill farms (a life entirely different from that of lowland farms), the sense of loneliness soon changes to one of friendliness. Many who have come to know them have found in the Cheviot Hills something that is lacking in many other districts of Britain, a full and exciting history giving weight to strong and enduring traditions. A knowledge and apprecia-tion of these traditions is but the prelude to that full enjoyment of the subtle and less obvious charms of the hills themselves.

The great Cheviot massif itself consists of several kinds of igneous rock that were thrust up in a molten state, in a series of volcanic outpourings, bursting through and spreading over the existing sedimentary rocks as a thick bed of lava. Later outpourings included a molten rock rich in gritty substances such as quartz and silica, and these, solidifying as granite, covered the tops of Cheviot, Comb Fell and Hedgehope. Except in a few places, such as Henhole and the Bizzle, deep ravines in the steep flanks of Cheviot, these granite outcrops rarely display themselves, and the hill sur-faces of the Cheviots as a rule tend to be smooth. The hills are mainly con-ical in shape and they are mostly covered with grass, though this is pleasantly interspersed in many places with bracken. In other places, par-ticularly on the domed summits of the highest hills, the grass gives way to heather, cloudberry and other acid-loving plants.

The Cheviots are important shepherding country; indeed, looked at economically, sheep are practically the only reason for their existence (it is estimated that there are nearly a quarter of a million sheep in the Northumberland National Park). Two native breeds are to be seen on the hills, the short-wooled, white-faced, hornless species known as the Cheviot sheep, and the even more common horned, swarthy-visaged variety appropriately called the Blackface. Both breeds are crossed regularly with a larger, white-faced, thick-wooled breed named the Border Leicester (originally a native of south Northumberland) to com-bine the hardy strain of the hill breeds with the better meat-yielding qualities of the lowland stock.

Sheep farmlands are divided into two areas, the enclosed fields around the farmstead itself (the 'in-bye') and the much more extensive grazing land (the 'out-bye') reaching up to the hill tops and usually fenced or wall-ed round the perimeter. Life on a Cheviot hill farm may appear to the lowlander both hard and unvaried, but sheep can become a surprisingly interesting subject, and the shepherd gains, what the occasional visitor can never do, an unrivalled knowledge of the hills under every condition, that true knowledge which is the real basis for love of the hills. The shepherd is kept a great deal busier than may be expected; an average farm that I know of has normally about 2,000 sheep to care for. These have about 4,000 acres of land to range over, including a fair amount of heather; but as a practice is made of burning the heather about every three years, it is given a glossy top which the sheep relish.

No-one who has walked (and preferably slept out) on the hills, or who has fished the clear burns, will forget the harsh guttural bleating of the sheep in the evening, as the flock, seeking fresh grass or heather, pursues its way to the heights (the path of a sheep is naturally upward), or in the early morning, when the shepherds come out to 'gather', driving the flock, with the aid of their wonderfully clever Border collies (the best and most popular of sheep dogs), down to the fresher, sweeter grass of the valleys.

Though there is less to do in winter, conditions then can be very exact-ing, and considerable care needs to be exercised in hard weather if large numbers of sheep are not to be lost. Some sheep are almost bound to perish in drifts of snow each winter, despite the valiant efforts of the shepherds, who may spend many days in finding them and digging them out, and others will inevitably succumb to the sickness caused by exposure to the damp. Sheep can endure practically any amount of cold as long as the weather be dry, but they soon go under when it turns excessively wet. Others are affected by snow-blindness or 'staggers', as it is called. Outly-ing farmsteads may themselves be snowed up for several weeks in the winter; the farm already mentioned was completely cut off from the out-side world for about 17 weeks during the severe winter of 1940–41, and for about 11 weeks during the very bad blizzard of early 1947.

The isolation of many of these outlying farms is exemplified by Uswayford, the last farm on the Usway Burn (a principal feeder of the Coquet) and one of several 'last farms in England'. It is 3 miles from the nearest road (it was 8 miles before the road was extended up Coquetdale), 4 miles from the nearest school at Barrowburn, 10 miles from the nearest inn and the nearest shop (though groceries are actually brought from

Wooler, 25 miles away, to Barrowburn and carted up by the farmer himself), 12 miles from the nearest telegraph office (there is a small post office at Barrowburn), 20 miles from the nearest regular bus service and 35 miles from the nearest accessible railway station.

But even these outlying farms are not as solitary as they were. It is not so many years since the road up the Coquet ended at Linsheeles, not far above Alwinton, and only a cart-road continued up the dale to the highest farm, some 12 miles on. The farm-roads up the Harthope, College and Bowmont valleys have given place to roads with tarred surfaces in recent years, though that in the College Valley is still privately owned. The road in the Breamish Valley extends only about half-way through the valley, and the upper part is privately owned and inaccessible to cars. And these are the principal valleys, the main arteries of the hills, as it were. Some of the remoter farms can be reached only by footpath or unmade-up cart-track.

Sheep sales take place at Wooler, Rothbury, Bellingham, Hexham and Carlisle, on the English side of the Border, and at Kelso and Hawick, among other places, on the Scottish. The sales begin in April and go on until October; as many as 100,000 sheep may change hands during this period, and 10,000 may be sold in a single sale. Here may be seen, according to the time of year, Cheviots and Blackfaces, Half-breds and Grayfaces (the Border Leicester cross), as well as Swaledales (which came from Yorkshire) and other 'foreign' breeds, rams (known in the North as 'tups'), ewes, lambs and gimmers (ewes between one and two years old). A good ram may fetch what appears to the uninitiated to be an exorbitant price.

Other interesting events that take place every year are the Border Shepherds' Shows at Yetholm (on the first Saturday in October) and at Alwinton (on the second Saturday). Both include important sheep shows, with classes representing the principal breeds (the most popular being the Blackface), as well as sheepdog trials, foot races and other athletic events, wrestling in the Cumberland and Westmorland style favoured in the Border, and (at Alwinton) a hound trail over an exacting ten-mile course round the hills enclosed by the Coquet.

Not least among the charms of the Cheviot Hills is the complete absence of the popular tourist atmosphere. Here, one feels, life is truly lived; the hills have a deeper function than to be a mere show-piece for the attraction of the unthinking visitor. This freedom from the common failing of more popular places is due partly to the comparative difficulty of access to the hills by the everyday means of travel. On the English side the most approachable of the villages on their fringes is 16 miles from any railway station, while others are considerably farther away. In addition, the linking bus services are often very infrequent, and some operate only on certain days of the week; the buses, in fact, cater for farm people visiting the nearest market rather than for visitors wishing to reach the hills. Even the rapid increase in popularity of the motor-car has not made the hills much more accessible.

Another reason why the Cheviots have been fortunate enough to escape being overrun by tourists is the lack of hotel and similar accommodation inside the area. Though there are hotels and inns in the villages around the edge of the hills, from which it is possible to strike into their recesses, there is absolutely no accommodation among the hills themselves. One can sometimes obtain food and a bed at the farmhouses, but few farmers make a habit of catering for visitors. Those seeking accommodation at farmhouses should, of course, make arrangements in advance wherever possible; it is obviously unfair to descend on some lonely and unsuspecting house (especially during the farmer's busiest months, May to August, when the young lambs have to be attended to) and expect to be provided with food and lodging.

The easiest and best way to explore the Cheviots is to follow up the valleys to the hills at their heads. The valleys mostly spread out like the spokes of a wheel from the main body of the hills. To the east flows the River Breamish, the head-reach of the River Till; to the north-east is the Harthope Burn, which lower down becomes the Wooler Water; to the north is the College Burn, which joins the Bowmont Water, on the north-west, to form the River Glen; and to the south are the Alwin and the Usway Burn (Chapter 5), descending towards Coquetdale.

For those coming from the south, via Newcastle, the easiest access to the Cheviot Hills is by the valley of the Breamish (pronounced 'Bremish' locally), the only one of the Cheviot burns to be distinguished by the name of river, though it is no larger than some of the others. Rising on Scotsman's Knowe, the southernmost buttress of Cheviot, it maintains a general direction eastward until it leaves the confines of the hills. To the north of Powburn, and beyond the river, a road turns off up the open valley to Ingram, a hamlet enchantingly situated at the boundary of the Northumberland National Park and the entrance to the fine gorge by which the Breamish pushes its way out of the hills. The restored church, mainly of the twelfth and thirteenth centuries, has a sturdy tower and narrow windows indicating that (like other churches in the Border) it was designed to be used for defence. The old school near by is now an information centre for the National Park.

Beyond Ingram the hills rise steeply on either hand, liberally dotted with hill-forts, settlements and other prehistoric remains, the only evidence of a civilisation that once flourished all over the Cheviots. One of the best of the hill-forts is on Brough Law, a steep-faced hill which forces the river to make a sharp bend from south to east. From below the hill the road strikes sharply up out of the restricted gorge to Greensidehill, below the broad southern slopes of Dunmoor Hill (1860 feet), one of the most distinctive of the Cheviot Hills, from its position on the edge of the group.

The public road up the Breamish Valley ends at Hartside, but a private farm-road descends to Linhope, hidden away among trees on a tributary burn, one of the most exquisite places in the Cheviots. Before walking down to the farmstead it is worth turning through a gate to find the late-prehistoric village of Greaves Ash, situated on a shelf of the hillside, and the most interesting of the settlements in the Cheviots. The village consists of three separate enclosures, the largest (to the west) containing a great number of hut-circles surrounded by a double rampart of granite blocks. The entrance to the outer rampart is not opposite that to the inner, but is displaced about 20 yards round the perimeter, so that a direct entry to the enclosure was impossible. The foundations of many of the dwellings, which varied in diameter from 11 to 27 feet, can still be discerned. The middle enclosure, on slightly higher ground, has no rampart, but has the best example of a hut dwelling, while the eastern enclosure, 100 yards farther on, occupies the ridge of the hill.

On the burn more than half a mile above the farm is Linhope Spout, the finest of the Cheviot waterfalls, cascading into a deep, rock-bound pool overhung by birches and surrounded by the steep, bracken-sided hills. Though slight in seasons of dry weather, the fall thunders down in an impressive manner when the burn is in spate.

From Alnhammoor, on the Breamish below Hartside, a cart-track ascends westward to regain the main valley before reaching the farm of Low Bleakhope (or Blakehope), where the Salter's Road (Chapter 5) comes down from Alnham. The track ends at High Bleakhope, the highest farm, but the old road (difficult to follow in places) climbs westward out of the upper reaches of the Breamish on its way towards Davidson's Linn, a charming waterfall, three-quarters of a mile above Uswayford, and thence to the Border at Cocklawgate.

The Newcastle-Wooler road, after crossing the Breamish, skirts the eastern flanks of the Cheviots, with good views towards Dunmoor Hill and Hedgehope. The fifteenth-century Percy's Cross, on the right of the road, commemorates the Battle of Hedgeley Moor, where in 1464 the Yorkists, commanded by Lord Montagu, defeated the Lancastrians under the Duke of Somerset and Sir Ralph Percy, who was slain. From Wooperton a road running south of Roddam Dene (where boulders and rounded pebbles brought down from the Cheviots by primeval flood waters can be seen) is continued by a track west to Threestoneburn House. This takes its name from a Bronze Age stone circle in the angle between two burns to the west of the farm. The circle, elliptical in shape and 39 yards long, comprises 13 monoliths, the largest over 5 feet long, of which only five now stand upright.

Wooler, a small market town on the last spur of a green foothill rising above the Wooler Water, a tributary of the Till, is the most convenient base for exploring the Cheviots as a whole. It is situated at the north-east edge of the group, overlooking the wide levels of Milfield Plain, which were once covered by a lake. Though it has an old-world appearance, the town has no buildings of any great antiquity, having been devastated by fire in 1722 and again in 1862, and its past history confirms its present peaceful existence. One of the baronies into which Northumberland was divided after the Norman Conquest, Wooler was granted by Henry I to the Muschamps, then among the strongest families in the North Country. Later it became the property of the Percys of Alnwick, from whom it passed to the Greys of Chillingham. But its only glimpse of any stirring event was the entry of the little band of Northumbrian Jacobites, led by General Forster and Lord Derwentwater, on their way to join the rising of 1715.

The upper part of the Wooler Water, emerging from the hills by a deep and narrow ravine, is known as the Harthope Burn, and its valley is not only the easiest to approach from Wooler, but has the advantage of leading into the very heart of the Cheviot Hills. The burn rises on the peaty saddle connecting Cheviot itself with Comb Fell and flows down between the major hill and Hedgehope; it therefore provides the most direct ascents of these, the highest of the Cheviots.

The road to the valley starts southward from Wooler, skirting the green foothills to Middleton Hall. Beyond this, at the top of a steep climb, a magnificent view opens suddenly up the long Harthope Valley, with Cheviot to the right and Hedgehope just in sight to the left, one of the most enchanting prospects in the Cheviots. On the east slopes of Brands Hill, which encloses the valley to the south, are the remains of stone huts of numerous Romano-British villages. Our road descends sharply to cross the Carey Burn, entering the National Park, then continues up the delightful main valley.

After penetrating rich pine plantations we reach the white farmhouse of Langleeford, where Walter Scott stayed in the autumn of 1791, imbibing the history and legends that he later turned to such good account. 'Behold a letter from the mountains', he wrote to a friend, 'for I am snugly settled here, in a farmer's house about six miles from Wooler, in the very centre of the Cheviot Hills, in one of the wildest and most romantic situations ... amidst places renowned by the feats of former days. ... My uncle drinks the whey here, as I do ever since I understood it was brought to his bedside every morning at six by a very pretty dairymaid. So much for my residence; all the day we shoot, fish, walk, and ride; dine and sup upon fish struggling from the stream, and the most delicious heath-fed mutton, barn-door fowls, poys (pies), milk-cheese, etc., all in perfection; and so much simplicity resides among these hills, that a pen, which could write at least, was not to be found about the house, though belonging to a considerable farmer, till I shot the crow with whose quill I wrote this epistle.' The goat's milk whey was a fashionable cure of the time at such places as Wooler and Rothbury.

At Langleeford the narrow road gives out, but a cart-road continues up the valley. Hedgehope (2343 feet; 'head of the valleys'), which has become the predominant feature to the south, is most easily climbed from this side. Second in height among the Cheviot Hills, it is the most outstanding, partly by reason of its distinctive conical shape and partly owing to its position near the edge of the group, making it visible from many places south of the Border. The exceptionally wide view, finer than that from Cheviot, embraces a great length of the Northumberland coast, with Holy Island, Bamburgh Castle, the Farne Islands and the towers of Dunstanburgh, as well as the wooded Chillingham Park, climbing to the fell-sandstone ridge culminating in Ros Castle, and a broad expanse of the Cheviots themselves. To the south are the Simonside Hills, and on a clear day the Pennines (farther south), Skiddaw in the Lake District, and Ettrick Forest and the Lammermuirs, in Scotland, can be seen. A descent may be made southward to Linhope Spout, above the Breamish Valley, or it is possible to walk over the adjoining Comb Fell (2132 feet) to the summit of Cheviot, though this involves much laborious slogging through a waste of peat hags.

The shortest ascent of Cheviot (2674 feet) starts at Langleeford Hope, the last farm in the valley. It is a lengthy but not a difficult climb. Cheviot (the second highest point in England outside the Lake District) can be seen from so many places in the Border that it might be expected to afford wide views, but this unfortunately is not so. The top of the mountain consists of a vast plateau, and views can be enjoyed only by walking round the edge of this. To make matters worse the plateau is covered by an enormous waste of fissured (and usually wet) peat hags, so that progress over it is at any time difficult and after heavy rain is not worth attempting. The best traverse of Cheviot is to ascend by Henhole from the College Valley and go down either to Langleeford or by the Bizzle.

Cheviot must be one of the most remote of English hills, not only in the sense of being far removed from any large centre of population, and from any means of public transport, but also in being among the least known and least ascended. One can spend whole days on these heights at almost any season of the year and yet meet scarcely another person, apart from an occasional shepherd. It is all the more surprising, then, to discover that Daniel Defoe, during his grand tour into Scotland in 1726, was prompted by a 'curiosity of no extraordinary kind' to make an expedition to the summit of what was then practically an unknown hill.

The College Valley may be reached most directly by walkers from Wooler by taking a pleasant lane and farm-road west to Commonburn House, then continuing by path, keeping to the south of Newton Tors. A splendid view of the valley opens up before the steep descent to Southernknowe. The northern entrance to the valley may be reached by

1 Hadrian's Wall: looking towards Housesteads
2 Housesteads (*Vercovicium*): the granary

3 *left* Hexham Priory: from the Market Place
4 Corbridge: 17th-century bridge over the Tyne
5 Berwick: the three bridges over the Tweed

6 Hedgehope: from the Cheviot
7 *opposite* Cragside, above the Coquet near Rothbury

8 *opposite* Alnwick Castle: from the river Aln
9 Hulne Priory: the Gothicised pele-tower
10 Newton Arlosh: the fortified church

11 *opposite, above* Warkworth Castle: from the river Coquet
12 *opposite, below* The Tweed near Melrose, with the Eildon Hills
13 Dunstanburgh Castle: the Lilburn Tower

14 The Farne Islands: the Pinnacles on Staple Island
15 Lindisfarne Castle: from Holy Island harbour
16 *opposite* Bamburgh: the great Norman castle

17 Kelso Abbey: with the Roxburgh Cloister
18 Carlisle Cathedral: from the south-west

19 *top left* Bewcastle: the Anglian cross
20 *top right* Jedburgh Abbey: reconstructed cloister doorway
21 Carrawburgh: altars in the Mithraic temple

22   Melrose Abbey: from the east
23   *opposite, top left* Alnwick Church: medieval effigies
24   *opposite, top right* Hulne Priory: stone figure of a monk
25   Chillingham Church: the Grey monument

26   Dryburgh Abbey: grave of Sir Walter Scott

the road west from Wooler, leaving the Coldstream road to ascend the narrowing valley of the River Glen, a tributary of the Till. The road runs below the flanks of Humbleton Hill, Harehope Hill and Yeavering Bell, the bold northern buttresses of the Cheviots.

Humbleton Hill (977 feet) is the best short ascent from Wooler. It shows as a rounded, bracken-covered cone with a distinctive cairn, and can be reached from the Commonburn House road or (more steeply) through the 'decayed' village of Humbleton, once a place of some importance, but now no more than a dozen cottages. The view from the hill top, largely because of its unrivalled position on the edge of the Cheviots, is one of the finest in the Border. On the lower slopes of the hill, on its northern side, was fought in 1402 the battle which history books still call Homildon Hill (this, or something near it, was the medieval spelling). The Earl of Douglas and his followers were returning from a successful foray into Northumberland, which they had penetrated as far as Newcastle, when they were surprised here by a force led by the Earl of Northumberland and his son, the redoubtable Hotspur. Though Douglas hurriedly took up a strong position, the skill of the English bowmen enabled them to rout the Scots. Their victory was wasted by an absurd quarrel with Henry IV over the disposal of the prisoners. The king demanded that they be surrendered to the Crown, but the Percys, upholding the unwritten feudal code, refused to give them up and this disagreement led to the revolt of the Percys in the following year that forms the main theme of Shakespeare's *Henry IV*.

Harehope Hill, the summit to the west of Humbleton Hill, can easily be reached from it. On the hill, not on the top, as usual, but on the shoulder by which it is joined to the main body of the moorlands, is an unusual hill-fort, square in plan, to accommodate its position, with ramparts once as much as 6 feet high. The fort was approached by a broad road from the east up the steep ravine of Monday Cleugh, the entrance passage cutting the walls at an oblique angle. On the north-west side, abutting against the outer wall and sheltered by an additional rampart, are the remains of many hut-circles.

Yeavering Bell (1182 feet), the next height of interest to the west, can be reached from Wooler over the moors or more directly, though more steeply, from the farmstead of Old Yeavering, at its northern foot. The hill is one of the most familiar of the Cheviots, due partly to its detached position at the edge of the group, but even more to its distinctive conical shape (hence the term 'bell'). It is well worth climbing for two reasons: it is an exceptionally fine view-point, much better than Cheviot and many higher elevations; and on the top is an Iron Age hill-fort of remarkable size and outstanding interest. The fort, elliptical in plan, is bounded by a dry-stone wall of which scarcely any courses now stand, these forming a tumbled rampart round the brow of the hill, while on three sides may be found the remains of gateways with their adjoining guard-chambers. Inside the area are numerous traces of hut-circles, of a horseshoe pattern with their openings facing south-east (in the traditional manner), and on the higher of the two summits is a cup-shaped depression surrounded by a ditch. For a prehistoric stronghold, this was a work of an exceptionally advanced order.

Old Yeavering stands near the site of a timber palace first built in the 6th century for the Kings of Northumbria, and the only one of its kind in Britain. The palace was greatly enlarged for King Edwin (616–33), when it included an unusual amphitheatre and a great hall 100 feet long. It was excavated in 1953-57, but the remains have been covered in. This was the *ad Gefrin* of Bede's *Ecclesiastical History*, and a tablet beside the road tells its history. Here in A.D. 627 the missionary Paulinus, who came with Ethelburga of Kent for her marriage with Edwin, converted the Northumbrians to Christianity, baptizing them for 36 days, it is said, in the River Glen close by.

A little farther up the Glen is Kirknewton, a secluded hamlet with an interesting church. The tower and nave were rebuilt after 1860, but the rest is of the thirteenth or early fourteenth century. The tiny chancel has walls that are less than 3 feet high, and from their top springs a pointed tunnel vault in the style of a pele-tower basement. To the south of the nave is a small transept of a similar character, and the church was obviously meant for defence. In the east wall of the nave is a crude relief, probably of the twelfth century, showing the Adoration of the Magi, who are attired in the dress of the time.

The road bridges the College Burn and ascends the valley of the Bowmont Water, shut in by steep, green hills from which there appears to be no exit. But it would be a mistake not to turn aside to explore the College Valley, the narrow entrance to which is almost hidden by the rounded hump of Hethpool Bell. The College Burn (the name seems to be derived from the Anglo-Saxon 'col-leche', a stream in boggy land) flows through perhaps the most beautiful of the Cheviot dales, whose charms are certainly not lessened by its being more inaccessible than most. The College Valley strikes right at the heart of the hills, its upper reaches dominated by the broad flanks of the 'muckle' Cheviot himself, to which it forms by far the best approach.

At the foot of the long, open part of the valley is the estate of Hethpool, and in the grounds of the house are the ivy-covered ruins of a fourteenth-century pele. Beyond Hethpool the road is private, and car-drivers who have no specific business in the valley must obtain permits in advance by writing to the Estate Office in Wooler. On Great Hetha (1129 feet), to the west, are the massive ramparts of an Iron Age hill-fort, while to the east the steep valley slopes lead up towards Newton Tors (1761 feet), the laborious ascent of which is repaid by the fine view of the valley and its enclosing hills. The large grove of trees, known as the Collingwood Oaks, that lines the foot of the Tors is said to have been planted by Admiral Lord Collingwood, the friend of Nelson and hero of Trafalgar, who owned the estate at Hethpool (though his duties prevented him from seeing his native county for many years). 'What I am most anxious about', he wrote in 1828, 'is the plantation of oak in the country. We shall never cease to be a great people while we have ships, which we cannot have without timber. . . . I plant an oak wherever I have a place to put it in.' But before his trees had grown to maturity we were building iron ships! Oak woods of this nature formerly covered the whole of the lower slopes of the Cheviots.

At Southernknowe the College receives the waters of the Lambden Burn, a tributary as large as the main burn itself. From the white farm of Dunsdale, in the Lambden Valley, starts one of the most interesting ascents of Cheviot, at first to the left of the Bizzle, a deep gash in the hillside whose bold crags can be seen high above, then following up the Bizzle Burn to its source, about a quarter of a mile from the summit mound. This route is even better for the descent, as it provides a quick and fairly easy way off Cheviot (particularly in mist) and the sheer crags on the west side look even finer from above.

The Border line traverses the high ridge to the west, between the College Valley and the parallel valley of the Bowmont Water, and several tracks link the two valleys, some of them following the courses of old drove roads. They mostly make for two crossings that were known in medieval times as the White Swire and the Pete Swire. Beyond Mounthooly, the last farm in the College Valley, the road dwindles to a track, and at the head of the long strath, at the mouth of a great corrie, this divides. The branch to the right ascends to the saddle of the Red Cribs, another old Border crossing, and goes over to Sourhope, in the Bowmont Valley. That to the left keeps alongside the burn as it turns abruptly towards the entrance to Henhole, a wild rock-bound gorge (frequented by climbers), easily the most impressive place of its kind in the Cheviots. It is advisable to keep to the right-hand side of the burn throughout the ascent, climbing above the charming waterfall known as the Three Sisters and passing directly under the great upstanding rock of Raven Crag. Above two more falls the ravine steepens considerably and takes a turn to the south. We emerge on to the peat hags and by following the College Burn to its source find ourselves less than a quarter of a mile south-west of the summit mound of Cheviot.

By skirting the hillside south of Henhole we can gain the Border ridge near Auchope Cairn (2382 feet), distinguished by four large cairns that look from below exactly like mountaineers struggling along the crest of its narrow ridge. Farther south-east is the west top of Cairn Hill (2419 feet), the highest elevation in the Cheviots extending at least partly into Scotland. About a quarter of a mile south-west of this (and south of the Border fence) is the Hanging Stone, an outcrop of fell-sandstone 17 feet high, named from its tilted appearance, not from any event in Border history, though this was the boundary mark between the East and Middle Marches.

The road we left to explore the College Valley goes on across the Border to the twin villages of Town and Kirk Yetholm, one on each side of the Bowmont Water, enchantingly placed just where the hills begin to fall away and the river leaves a confined glen for a somewhat wider strath. Kirk Yetholm, the older but smaller village, on the east bank, was long the 'capital' of the notorious gipsy clan of the Faas that flourished in the Border. A row of houses, on the other side of the green from the thatch-roofed Border Hotel, is known as Gipsy Row, and a small cottage above this was called the Gipsy Palace. Kirk Yetholm had an evil reputation in those days, when hordes of tinkers issued every spring and took to the road. Travellers gave it a very wide berth, for 'if a stranger showed in

Yetholm, it was oot aik sticks and bull pups'! But the 'dynasty' declined and the last 'queen', Esther Fall (or Faa) Blyth, was buried in the churchyard in 1883. The character of Meg Merrilees, in Scott's *Guy Mannering*, is said to have been taken from an earlier 'queen'.

Kirk Yetholm is at the northern end of the Pennine Way, which follows the Border line all the way from the Chew Green forts (Chapter 5) over Windy Gyle and Auchope Cairn (with an unnecessary divergence to the top of Cheviot) to reach the saddle between The Schil (1985 feet), topped by a mass of riven rocks, and Black Hag (1801 feet), before descending on the Scottish side to the valley of the Halter Burn. From here it completes its course over the north side of Staerough (the second syllable is pronounced as in 'loch'), the hill that stands up prominently behind Kirk Yetholm and is worth ascending for the view of the Bow-mont Valley and its enclosing hills, which, though not particularly high, are pleasantly diversified with clumps of trees.

Town Yetholm, on the other side of the valley, is not quite as 'primitive' as its neighbouring village, but it tones equally well into the landscape. It has a fine broad main street, with a green lined by sycamores and other trees, and a thatched roof or two, an unusual sight in the Border.

A fair road runs up the valley of the Bowmont Water to the se-questered farm of Belford, from which a good green track crosses the hills westward to Hownam (Chapter 11), on the Kale Water. Our road follows the narrowing valley eastward to Sourhope (the first syllable is soft), now an experimental centre of the Hill Farming Research Organisa-tion, on a tributary burn. A track ascends the burn from here to Schilgreen and a path thence goes over the Border between Black Hag and The Schil for Fleehope, below Mounthooly in the College Valley.

A branch road continues by the Bowmont Water to the junction of its two main feeders, the Cheviot Burn, which rises high up under Auchope Cairn, and the Kelsocleuch Burn, whose source is on the slopes of Windy Gyle. (The Cheviot Burn appears from the map to be mis-named, as it is separated from the mountain not only by Auchope Cairn but by the deep valley of the upper College; but as seen from the Bowmont it does look as though it rises on Cheviot itself.) The hills on the Scottish side of the Border, though not so high as their English counterparts, are broken up in an engaging fashion by the feeders of the Bowmont, and this, together with a greater degree of cultivation, gives the Scottish side of the Cheviots a character different from, though certainly not less attractive than, the English side.

The branch to the left at the head of the Bowmont Water leads to the farm of Cocklawfoot, the starting point of the old drove road of Clennell Street (Chapter 5). This was one of the recognised routes over the hills between Scotland and England, and Cocklawgate, the Border crossing (known in medieval times as Hexpethgate), was a meeting place of the Lords Wardens of the Middle March. The old road descends over Hazely Law to the Usway Burn, with a branch to Uswayford.

The other branch from the Bowmont leads to Kelsocleuch, the highest farm, a base for the ascent of Windy Gyle (2032 feet), whose massive gable-like form fills the valley head. The fourth in height of the Cheviot Hills, it commands a splendid view of the country on both sides of the Border. The huge pile of stones on the summit, probably a Bronze Age burial mound, is known as Russell's Cairn. It was named after Sir Francis Russell, who lost his life at Hexpethgate in 1585, in one of those unfortunate affrays into which the meetings of the Wardens of the Marches all too frequently deteriorated.

CHAPTER SEVEN

From Alnwick to Chillingham

Travelling northward along the Great North Road from Newcastle, we see very little at first to convey the impression that we are on the verge of the historic and romantic Borderland. Beyond Morpeth, it is true, views begin to open up of the the jagged ridge of the Simonsides and the more distant rounded domes of the Cheviots, yet such views, though greatly encouraging, are not in themselves sufficient to instil that unique and pervasive atmosphere that is inherent in the Border Country. But as we leave the main road to enter Alnwick (pronounced 'An-nik') through the low, narrow archway of the fifteenth-century Hotspur Gate, the sole surviving part of the medieval town defences, we are projected suddenly and most effectively into the presence of a more austere yet more robust past.

The approach to Alnwick from whatever direction is indeed impressive. The Great North Road from Berwick and Scotland dips to the famous Lion Bridge over the River Aln, with its view of the walls and battlemented towers of Alnwick Castle. Entering by the Wooler road, we are confronted by the imposing gatehouse of the castle and the stout flanking turrets of its protective barbican. The road from Rothbury descends steeply from the high windswept moor straight to the old-world market place.

Alnwick, one of the most interesting places in Northumberland, is a delightful, unspoilt grey-stone market town, with intricate streets, charmingly placed above the south side of the Aln valley. I have always thought that it, and not Newcastle, should rightly be the county town, though Hexham also might stake a claim. Newcastle, of course, is easily accessible from almost every part of Northumberland and is the chief centre of commerce and industry, and these no doubt are the deciding factors, apart from mere size; but Alnwick and Hexham both retain the essence of the largely agricultural nature of the county.

Alnwick owes its interest principally to the presence of its castle, the ancestral home of the powerful and historic house of Percy, Earls and Dukes of Northumberland, standing at the north end of the town, on a steep bank overlooking the Aln. Though now indissolubly connected with the name of Percy, the castle did not become associated with that family until early in the fourteenth century. The barony of Alnwick had been granted by William the Conqueror, says tradition, to Gilbert Tisonne or de Tesson, his standard-bearer at the Battle of Hastings. It is not known whether Tisonne threw up the original foundations of the castle, but in any case the estate passed soon after 1096 to Ivo de Vesci or Vescy, one of a powerful Norman family, and the earliest parts of the present castle were begun before he died in about 1134. His daughter married Eustace FitzJohn, created Baron of Alnwick, who completed the building of the castle before his death in 1157.

Fitzjohn's son took his mother's name of De Vesci and this family held the property until the death of the last of the legitimate line in 1297; it then passed to the Percys in a way that curiously illustrates the manners of the period. William de Vesci had a natural son and he left the property in trust for him with Anthony Bek, Bishop of Durham, described as the 'proudest lord in Christendom'. The bishop, revealing a character much too common among the ecclesiastics of his time, neglected his charge and in 1309 sold the castle to Henry de Percy, putting the purchase money, it is believed, in his own pocket.

The Percys, who took their name from a village in Normandy, first came over to England with William the Conqueror, receiving grants of land in Yorkshire and elsewhere. The De Vescis had already built the original stone keep, but Henry Percy and his son, who succeeded him in 1315, replaced this by one more suitable as a feudal residence at the same time as they strengthened the defences by adding the strong flanking towers to the walls. Such measures were urgently necessary, for these were the dark days after the disastrous English defeat at Bannockburn. The Scots harried the whole of Northumberland and safety was to be found only in the shadow of powerful castle or fortified town.

Of the many warlike Percys who followed, the most celebrated was

'Harry Percy, that Hotspur of the North,' as Shakespeare calls him in *Henry IV*, making him the rival of the young Prince Hal, who, in the play, kills Hotspur at the Battle of Shrewsbury, in 1403. Though Hotspur did lose his life on that occasion, the future Henry V was then only 16, and history has no record of his killing Hotspur, who in fact had previously acted as his military adviser. The character of Hotspur has been made famous by the passage in *Henry IV* where Prince Hal is describing his rival: 'he that kills me some six or seven dozen of Scots at a breakfast, washes his hands, and says to his wife, "Fie upon this quiet life! I want work." "O my sweet Harry," says she, "how many hast thou killed to-day?" "Give my roan horse a drench", says he; and answers "Some fourteen", an hour after; "a trifle, a trifle." '

The Percys seem to have had a flair for getting themselves involved in unsuccessful causes, and the castle was frequently surrendered to the Crown. Hotspur's father, the fourth Percy of Alnwick and created Earl of Northumberland, was slain in 1409 at Bramham Moor while opposing Henry IV. The second Earl (the son of Hotspur) fell at the Battle of St Albans in 1455, and four of this earl's sons also lost their lives in the Wars of the Roses. The third Earl was killed in 1461 at the Battle of Towton, when the Lancastrian cause which the Percys had espoused collapsed; the fourth was murdered at Thirsk in 1489 while trying to enforce an unpopular tax imposed by Henry VII. The fifth Earl, called 'the Magnificent', was the first for many generations to die in bed; the sixth was unfortunate enough to be a lover of Anne Boleyn, whom Henry VIII already had his eye on; his nephew and successor was executed at York in 1572 for his part in a Northern Catholic rebellion against Elizabeth I. The eighth Earl, his Protestant brother, was found dead in bed in 1585 in the Tower of London, killed by a pistol shot fired, so his enemies said, by his own hand; the ninth, the 'Wizard Earl', was sent to the Tower for his supposed complicity in the Gunpowder Plot, but after 15 years was released on the payment of the enormous fine of £20,000.

After this the earls ceased to live in Northumberland, and in 1682 the estate passed by marriage to the sixth Duke of Somerset. The only daughter and heiress of the seventh Duke married a Yorkshire baronet, Sir Hugh Smithson, who changed his name to Percy and became Earl of Northumberland in 1750. Much of the castle had fallen into ruin in the seventeenth century and it remained in this condition until about 1755, when the Earl began a considerable restoration, to the designs of Robert Adam, who remodelled the castle internally in the pseudo-Gothic style which was becoming fashionable. The work was completed in 1766, the year in which the earl was created the first Duke of Northumberland. In 1854 the fourth Duke, influenced by contemporary tastes and employing Anthony Salvin as architect, undertook a second extensive restoration, converting the castle into a stately mansion that will bear comparison with any of the other great houses in the country.

Though the castle has experienced too drastic a restoration, it remains, externally at least, an outstanding example of a medieval fortress on a grand scale. The great extent of the fortifications, with their bold flanking towers and formidable encircling walls, dominated by the huge soaring mass of the keep, places Alnwick among the very finest strongholds in England, with Windsor, Dover, Arundel, Warwick, Durham and Bamburgh, for instance.

The castle is entered through an impressive fourteenth-century gatehouse, defended on the outside by a second gatehouse, or barbican, added in about 1440 by the second earl of Northumberland. Over the archway of this is the Percy shield, with a lion rampant and the Percy motto, *Esperance ma Comforte*. On the top of the gatehouse and barbican, the Abbot's Tower and the keep are small armed figures in various war-like attitudes. It is commonly believed that they were so placed with the intention of confusing an attacker, but in reality they were probably no more than decoration. The existing figures were put up only during the restoration of the first Duke, but presumably they take the place of earlier ones, as such figures are to be seen on Bothal Castle, on the Wansbeck, and formerly surmounted the old Clock Tower fronting the market place in Morpeth.

Alnwick is a remarkable example of the development from the early Norman 'motte-and-bailey' type of castle. This consisted of an earthen mound (usually man-made) surmounted by a 'keep', originally of timber, and surrounded by a bailey or courtyard enclosed by a palisade and ditch. The palisade was eventually replaced by a stone wall and the timber keep by one of stone. The bailey at Alnwick is divided into two approximately equal parts: the Outer Bailey, between the keep and the gatehouse, and the Middle Bailey, reached from the Outer Bailey by a second gatehouse called the Middle Gateway. These open courtyards were intended mainly for the exercise of the military forces and the retention of prisoners. The wall surrounding the baileys is reinforced by numerous towers and smaller intermediate fortifications called garrets (from the French *guérite*, a turret). Though many are rebuilt or restored, their names still have the authentic ring of some medieval ballad. To the north-west of the keep is the Falconer's Tower, rebuilt by the fourth Duke, then come the Abbot's Tower, at the north-west angle, and the Western Garret, both of the fourteenth century. To the south of the gatehouse and barbican are Avener's Tower (a garret), the Clock Tower (rebuilt in 1755–66) and the Auditor's Tower (on the south wall). Beyond the Middle Gateway are the Warder's Tower (restored in 1854–65), the fourteenth-century Eastern Garret, and the Record Tower (rebuilt in 1885); and on the north of the Outer Bailey are the site of the Ravine Tower (probably demolished in the seventeenth century), the so-called Hotspur's Seat (an early-fourteenth-century watch-tower) and the unspoilt Constable's Tower and the Postern Tower, both of the early fourteenth century. The last now contains a small but good collection of antiquities, mostly British and Roman.

The keep, between the Outer and Middle Baileys, encloses the small Inner Ward or Bailey, the most interesting part of the medieval work, bounded on one side by the State Apartments and on the other by the Inner Gatehouse, with its imposing octagon towers. The outer and inner doorways of this are the only surviving parts of the twelfth-century keep, the inner showing typically Norman chevron or zigzag moulding. Under the archway are doors admitting to guard-chambers, and below one of these is a gloomy underground prison. In the ward is the fourteenth-century draw-well, with the original wooden pole and wheels for winding up the buckets.

The State Apartments were converted to their present form by Salvin for the 4th and 5th Dukes, the decoration being completed in 1865, and little is to be seen of Robert Adam's work. They contain portraits of the Percys, paintings by Italian and other masters, including a landscape of the castle in the eighteenth century by Canaletto, and some elaborate eighteenth-century French furniture. The Library holds many fine early manuscripts and printed books. In the former Stables, near the Clock Tower, is kept the splendid state coach of 1825. The charming well-wooded park, through which the Aln flows, was refashioned in about 1765 by 'Capability' Brown, who planted many of the groves and copses. A fine view of it can be obtained from the terrace on the north side of the castle.

Alnwick was fortified in the mid-fifteenth century by the second Earl of Northumberland; previously, as an open town, it had suffered from the attacks of the marauding Scots. Evidence of the Percys is to be seen everywhere. The tall Tenantry Column at the southern entrance to the town is surmounted by a lion with a stiff, extended tail, one of the Percy emblems. It was put up by grateful tenants in 1816 to commemorate the liberality of the second Duke of Northumberland in reducing their rents. On the outer face of the Hotspur Gate is the Percy lion rampant (now almost defaced), and the stiff-tailed lion makes its appearance again on the Lion Bridge over the Aln, built by John Adam (brother of Robert) in 1773.

The broad Bondgate Within (i.e. 'within' the Hotspur Gate) is the main street of Alnwick. It runs east of the Market Place, a cobbled square with the medieval market cross. On the west side of this is the Town Hall, built in 1771, and on the south side is the Northumberland Hall, an assembly hall given to the town in 1826 by the third Duke. To the south-west is St Michael's Pant, a fountain or covered well, probably of medieval origin, topped by a carving of 1765 showing St Michael slaying the Dragon. Such pants, as they are called in the Border, are a familiar feature in Scotland, but less common on the English side, though Alnwick has six in all. Bailiffgate, the broad tree-lined street facing the castle barbican, has some of the many houses of the eighteenth and early nineteenth centuries to be found in Alnwick. Pottergate Tower, on the hill to the south of the street, is not part of the original fortifications, but was rebuilt in 1768.

Bailiffgate leads to the fine parish church, one of the only three examples in Northumberland (the others are Norham and Newcastle Cathedral) of a church having both north and south aisles extending the whole length of the nave and chancel. The nave arcades are of the fourteenth century, but most of the church was rebuilt after 1464 (when Henry VI granted tolls to the town) and has interesting tracery in the Perpendicular style. On a capital in the chancel is the crescent enclosing a fetterlock, another of the Percy emblems, first used apparently by the fourth Earl of Northumberland, who succeeded in 1469. At the east end of the south aisle is an unusual stairway, now ascending only to the roof, though formerly leading to a chamber remains of which can be seen outside the church. This was popularly believed to be a lookout tower to spy possible movements of Scottish invaders, but it probably served as an occasional residence for one of the chantry priests who officiated in the chapel below. Similar chambers existed in Yorkshire and elsewhere. The fifteenth-century west tower is remarkable for its massive stepped buttresses.

Football is still played in the streets of the town every year on Shrove Tuesday. Alnwick Fair, first held, it is said, in 1291, was revived in 1968 and is a colourful festival running for a week at the end of June and the beginning of July, with a traditional market each day and the townsfolk dressed in eighteenth-century costume.

Malcolm's Cross, hidden in a wood over half a mile north of the Lion Bridge, near the junction of the new by-pass with the Great North Road, marks the spot where Malcolm Canmore, King of Scotland, was killed, while invading Northumberland in 1093. Another monument, a stone put up in about 1860, indicates the place where William the Lion was captured, in 1174, on his way to besiege Alnwick Castle. This stands over a quarter-mile west of the castle, near the Forest Lodge to Hulne Park, the largest park in Northumberland and comparable in beauty with such better-known estates as Chatsworth and Castle Howard. The Northumberland County Show is held here every year, in June. The park is the property of the Duke of Northumberland, but those who obtain passes from the estate office in the castle are readily permitted to walk through it, though no cars are allowed. Just inside a second entrance, reached from the church by another bridge over the Aln, is a late fourteenth-century gatehouse bearing the arms of the Percys. This is the sole remnant of Alnwick Abbey, founded by the De Vescis in 1147 for Premonstratensian canons, an order established by St Norbert at Prémontré in France in 1119.

A road from the Forest Lodge and a footpath from Alnwick Abbey lead through the delightfully wooded park for about 1½ miles to the secluded ruins of Hulne Priory, the finest and best-preserved example in England of a friary of the Carmelites or White Friars (as they were often called, from the colour of their vestments) and one of the two oldest. It was established in about 1240 by the father of John de Vesci (who recorded the event in a charter), at about the same time as the friary at Aylesford, in Kent, now much restored and occupied again by Carmelites. The remains of Hulne Priory stand on a green shelf a little above the Aln, a position which enhances its setting in the wooded park. The remains have suffered through alterations made in about 1777 by the first Duke of Northumberland in the belief that he was improving their appearance. They are surrounded by a wall that appears to be original, though the battlements and turrets with which this was once reinforced have been removed. The church is similar to other churches of the Carmelites in that it consists only of a nave and chancel, without aisles, but the most interesting and the best preserved part of the priory is the sturdy tower added by the fourth Earl of Northumberland in 1488 as a refuge for the friars against the onslaughts of the Scots. Among English monasteries, only Lindisfarne Priory has a stronghold of this nature attached to it.

On the other side of the Aln, three-quarters of a mile south-west and well seen from Hulne Priory, is Brizlee Hill, covered by a thick growth of pines. Above these rises the top of Brizlee Tower, built by the first Duke in 1781 and commanding a wonderful view over the park and the surrounding countryside as far as the sea and the Cheviot Hills. To the north-west stretches a long ridge of the fell-sandstone that is such a prominent feature in the landscape of this part of Northumberland.

The road from Alnwick skirting the north side of Hulne Park ascends through a valley in the fell-sandstone to Eglingham (pronounced 'Ej-'), a flower-decked village which has a restored church, partly in the Early English style of the thirteenth century, but with a Gothic seventeenth-century chancel. Farther on, the road runs between the sandstone escarpment and the Breamish, which has here emerged from its valley in the Cheviots. On the hill above the hamlet of Old Bewick are the distinctive ramparts of a remarkable Iron Age hill-fort forming two connected circles in plan, rather like a pair of spectacles. Perhaps one circular fortification was an extension of the other. The small towerless church of Old Bewick, half a mile north beside the Kirk Burn, is a Norman structure, with the original arches to the chancel and the apse, though this was altered to a square end in the fourteenth century. The church belonged to Tynemouth Priory from about 1110 onwards.

At Bewick Bridge, the Breamish changes its name to the Till. A lane on the right ascends the escarpment to Ros Castle (1035 feet), the highest point on this section of fell-sandstone, topped by the denuded remains of another hill-fort. The summit was presented to the National Trust in 1936 as a memorial to Viscount Grey of Fallodon, the Foreign Minister who was even better known as a fisherman and naturalist, with whom it was a favourite view-point. It faces a broad expanse of the rounded Cheviot Hills in one direction, and in the other can be seen a long stretch of the coast, with Holy Island, Bamburgh Castle and the Farnes.

Among the trees below the hill are the towers of Chillingham Castle, a fine example of a type of fortification that developed in the North of England during the fourteenth century. This consisted of four massive corner towers connected by curtain walls that had the domestic apartments built against them on the inside. At Chillingham these connecting ranges were rebuilt on a more elaborate scale in about 1625. The castle first belonged to the Herons, but on that family dying out, in 1400, it passed to the Greys, the most powerful of Northumbrian families after the Percys, and in 1701 it came by marriage to the Bennet family, made Earls of Tankerville in 1714. The middle section of the north wing, with the principal entrance, was burned down during the Second World War, when the Army was in occupation, but has been rebuilt in its previous style. The present Earl, however, lives in California and the castle is threatened with demolition.

The church of Chillingham, in the small, secluded village near the castle gate, is basically of the twelfth and thirteenth centuries, though it has suffered from an all-too-common Victorian 'restoration'. The slope on which it is built necessitated the chancel being raised five steps above the nave. The church is worth visiting for the magnificent table-tomb of Sir Ralph Grey, the first of that family to own Chillingham Castle, who died in 1443. On the top are effigies of Sir Ralph and his wife, and round the sides are figures of saints and angels, a rare medieval survival, on a sumptuous monument that is without peer in the Border.

In the great park of Chillingham, which extends along the steep slopes of the fell-sandstone escarpment, roam the last herd of genuinely wild cattle in England. The cattle, which are believed to have remained pure for at least 700 years, still inhabit the park where they were originally found; in fact, they may be said to have preceded the park, which was enclosed in about 1250 by building a wall some 7 miles long round a tract of natural, not to say beautiful, country, including the 'chase' that was the home of the herd. The enclosure, a mixture of moorland, woodland and pasture, still retains today a great deal of its pristine wildness, and is the foremost park in the Border for rugged grandeur, as Hulne Park is for more homely beauty.

The Chillingham cattle are distinguished primarily by being pure white (or as near pure white as is possible). Otherwise the first impression of them may be a little disappointing, as, apart from this characteristic, they look from a distance very much like any other cattle. Nearer inspection, however, reveals a number of marked differences. The horns are in the shape of a crescent and are all set at the same angle, standing up from the top of the head instead of growing from in front of the ears, and they have black 'thimble' tips. The cattle all have black muzzles, and the inside of the ear is of a distinctive red colour. The older beasts also develop red 'cheeks', patches of a ruddy colour that extend from in front of the ear to about half-way towards the muzzle. The bulls are somewhat dingier than the cows in colour, a feature which is accentuated by their habit of rolling themselves in the sandy earth of the park.

The Chillingham cattle are slightly smaller than domestic cattle, and they are both shorter and slimmer in the leg. As a consequence, they run considerably faster; in fact, their turn of speed is really surprising. But they are wild only in the sense of being absolutely undomesticated; indeed they are normally of a very timid disposition. They are easily scared by unusual noises and movements; they will, for instance, move off quickly at the cry of a child and they are terrified of running dogs. At the sight of a fox they will race off in a bunch, their horns grating together as they stumble against each other. At most times it is perfectly safe to approach within a hundred yards of them, but during the season when the bulls do battle to select a leader, it is dangerous to draw near the herd. This event, which usually begins towards the end of July and may go on for more than a week, is heralded by a stentorian trumpeting on the part of the bulls.

In breeding, the cattle display a number of characteristics which differentiate them from domestic animals. The cow will leave the herd when it is about to calve, making a form like that of a hare for the reception of the young calf, and it will not permit any member of the herd to approach the calf. If a calf is taken by surprise, it will cower down to the ground in an attempt to conceal itself, like a hare in a form.

The cattle are perfectly undomesticated in their habits and will not allow themselves to be interfered with by man, not even by the warden of the cattle himself. They will partake of hay which he leaves out during very bad weather, but they will not touch artificial feeding-stuff, whatever the weather. As a result of the exceptionally fierce blizzard of early 1947 the cattle suffered severely; 20 animals were lost, some through pneumonia and other after-effects, so that the herd was reduced to 13, of which eight, fortunately, were cows. For nearly 18 months after this dis-aster not a single cow calved, and fears for the survival of the herd were expressed. But in the August of 1948 two calves were born and faith in the herd's fertility was restored. Since that time the herd has generally in-creased in strength and by January, 1976, the numbers had grown to 58 of which 30 were cows.

An alarming threat to the herd was posed by the outbreak of foot and mouth disease in Northumberland in 1966. If the cattle had caught the disease they would inevitably have been destroyed. Happily, they did not catch it, and to combat this possibility in the future a reserve herd of two cows and a bull has been established 'somewhere in Scotland'. On his death in 1971 the eighth Earl of Tankerville bequeathed the ownership of the herd to a new body, the Chillingham Wild Cattle Association, through whom arrangements can be made to see the cattle, under the guidance of the warden.

To the north of Chillingham, the fell-sandstone range is broken up into a series of sharp, detached escarpments with evocative names: Chatton-park Hill, Lyham Hill, Bowden Doors, Dancing Green Hill, Cockenheugh, Greensheen Hill, Shepherdskirk Hill and the Kyloe Hills. Roads crossing the range lead down the easier dip slope to the east to reach the Great North Road in the neighbourhood of Belford (Chapter 9).

To the west of the main escarpment of the fell-sandstone is a shorter, parallel range of similar hills, cut through by the Till below Chatton. To the north of Wooler (Chapter 6) and of the junction of the Wooler Water with the Till, this rises to a broad moorland culminating in Dod Law (655 feet), the highest point of the range, commanding from its isolated position an amazingly wide view of the Cheviot Hills and the level valley of the Till. On top of the hill, not on the low outcrops that face the Cheviots, but on flat slabs of rock behind them, are several mysterious cup-and-ring sculptures of the kind that we found at Lordenshaws (Chapter 5).

Doddington, at the west foot of Dod Law, has an Early English church with the chancel arranged, very unusually, at the west end. But it seems that this chancel was originally a vestibule or west chamber, and the orthodox chancel was at the east end. After the orthodox chancel was rebuilt in 1838, on a larger scale, it became part of the nave, and consequently the west chamber was converted into a new chancel. In a farmyard is a pele tower built in 1584, only 19 years before the Union of the Crowns and perhaps the latest genuine example in the Border.

Roads lead down the east side of the Till Valley towards Ford (Chapter 10). One road, along the foot of the fell-sandstone moorlands, passes near Roughting Linn (pronounced 'Row-' as in 'now'), a pretty waterfall in a wooded ravine. On a sandstone rock nearby are further good examples of the cup-and-ring sculptures. The exposed road from Wooler and Doddington to Berwick passes the restored church of Ancroft, which has a pele-like tower of about 1300 with a vaulted basement and obviously built for defence.

CHAPTER EIGHT

The Lordly Strand of Northumberland

The seaboard of Northumberland has a tendency to be flat, as travellers by the Great North Road or the main-line railway between London and Edinburgh will have noticed, and this has perhaps influenced their opinion about the whole of this part of the Borderland. But to those who have troubled to explore the coast from the Coquet to the Tweed, any deficiency felt in the lack of long stretches of high cliff or striking rock scenery is more than offset by the extent and firmness of the sands (Swinburne's 'lordly strand of Northumberland'), the absorbing natural history of Holy Island and the Farne Islands offshore, and the outstanding interest and impressive settings of its medieval remains, the castles of Warkworth, Dunstanburgh and Bamburgh and the priory of Lindisfarne.

Warkworth is a convenient starting point for the exploration of the North Northumberland coast. The village lies seven miles south-east of Alnwick, on the lowest of the numerous bends of the Coquet, almost within sound of the sea. The approach from Alnwick leads down through a defile enclosed by trees to a new bridge beside the beautiful, if narrow, fourteenth-century bridge of two bold arches, once defended on its southern side by a gatehouse, long in ruins. The sweep of the Coquet here in its deep ravine, lined by low sandstone outcrops overhung with rich woods, is exceptionally entrancing. So deep-set is the river that neither it nor the village climbing from its bank is visible from the surrounding country. From a distance the great castle at the head of the main street appears to stand in solitary state on an undulating plateau.

The church of Warkworth, standing alongside the river, was first built for Ceolwulf, King of Northumbria (to whom Bede dedicated his great history), and it was one of the five churches which he granted to Lindisfarne when he retired to that monastery. The present church was begun in about 1130 by Richard de Aurival, chaplain of Henry I, and this Norman structure, consisting of nave and chancel, has survived almost in its entirety. Though outwardly less impressive than the churches at Alnwick and Bamburgh, and even that at Norham, Warkworth church is at least as interesting and beautiful internally. In the north wall of the nave are five characteristic Norman windows, while the richly-decorated chancel arch has a fan-like moulding which may well be unique. The chancel has a vaulted ceiling (a feature not usually met with so early), with zigzag moulding on its diagonal ribs, perhaps inspired by Durham Cathedral. The tower was added in about 1200 and the south arcade and aisle were built early in the fourteenth century; in the aisle is a finely-carved effigy of a knight, of about 1330. The fourteenth-century spire is the only medieval example in Northumberland, except that at Newbiggin-by-the-Sea. Over the porch is a fifteenth-century 'parvis' or priest's room, the only one in the county; in it Sir Walter Besant is said to have written part of his novel about Northumberland, *Dorothy Forster*.

The village of Warkworth is crowded on to a narrow peninsula almost encircled by the Coquet, and it has many houses of the eighteenth and early nineteenth centuries in and around the market place, south of the church, and along the road to the bridge. The broad main street mounts steeply from the market place to the neck of the peninsula, defended by the magnificent castle. Since it has not suffered at the hands of the restorer like the castles at Alnwick and Bamburgh, this remains one of the most important examples of medieval military architecture in England, described by Hamilton Thompson as 'the epitome of the history of the castle from its Norman origin to its practical identification in the later Middle Ages with the large manor house'.

The earliest castle here, of the usual motte-and-bailey type, was begun by Robert de Mowbray, the first Norman Earl of Northumberland, late in the eleventh century. Its position, strong but by no means impregnable, determined that its shape (an irregular triangle, with the motte rising from its northern apex) should conform to the ground on which it is situated. The outer wall (enclosing two large wards or baileys) was begun by Henry, son of David I of Scotland and in 1139 created Earl of Northumberland, who had been granted the county. Robert FitzRoger, a descendant of Eustace FitzJohn of Alnwick, added the gatehouse in the centre of the south wall (in 1199) and the Carrickfergus Tower (named from his Irish property) projecting from the south-west corner. After the castle had been twice besieged by the Scots, in 1327, the Grey Mare's Tail Tower in the eastern wall was built, the keep was reconstructed on the motte and the gatehouse was enlarged into a tower. This last, the principal entrance to the castle and still one of the best-preserved parts, was of supreme importance, as the south wall, which faced the only level approach to the castle, had been protected only by a ditch. The castle soon after came into the hands of Edward III, but he sold it in 1332 to Henry Percy, second Lord of Alnwick, whose family retained the property almost continuously for over 600 years, and indeed until the sixteenth century regarded it as important as their castle at Alnwick.

The Outer and Inner Wards were separated by a collegiate church founded in the early fifteenth century by the first Earl of Northumberland, but of this only the lower courses now survive. The present keep, described in a survey of 1538 as a 'marvellous proper dongeon', was erected in about 1400 on the site of the earlier keeps. It is of unorthodox design, the ground plan consisting of a large square with a semi-octagonal bay projecting from each face. On the north side, facing down to the village, is a well-preserved Percy lion, and reaching beyond the full height of the building is an unusual light well. The principal rooms, on the first floor, include the Great Hall, extending upward to the roof, and an ornate chapel with a three-sided apse and an unusual gallery, entered from a similar gallery in the hall. In the early sixteenth century the keep was converted into a dwelling house by the seventh Earl of Northumberland, though it still remained a fortification, a dual arrangement unparalleled in England.

At the same time as the new keep was built, the Great Hall at the southern end of the courtyard was refronted. The existence of two Halls (indeed, two sets of domestic quarters) is due to the keep having been designed originally as a defence work, while the range of buildings in the south-west corner first constituted the living apartments of the family. The Lion Tower, displaying a weathered Percy lion, with a crescent collar, and the motto *Esperance*, was built in about 1480 by heightening the entrance porch to the Great Hall. The castle fell into ruin in the late sixteenth century, during the troublous times of the eighth and ninth Earls of Northumberland. Shakespeare laid several scenes of *Henry IV*, Part I, in Warkworth Castle, which he calls 'this worm-eaten hall of ragged stone', a description which may have been applicable in his day, but certainly wasn't in Hotspur's.

About half a mile upstream from the castle and reached only by a ferry-boat threading one of the most exquisite reaches of the Coquet, is the Hermitage, a complete dwelling carved out of the sandstone cliff, and undoubtedly the finest of its kind in England. It can be reached only by the ferry, as those hiring pleasure-boats on the river are not permitted to set foot ashore near the entrance. Practically nothing is known of the history of the dwelling; its earliest record is the appointment of Thomas Barker as 'chaplain' in 1487 by the fourth Earl of Northumberland. The hermitage is the subject of a famous ballad by Bishop Percy (compiler of the *Reliques of Ancient Poetry*) for whose account, however, there exists no historical validity.

The retreat is gained by a flight of steps and entered through a small porch, inside which, looking up, one could formerly distinguish a Latin inscription which told that 'Tears have been my bread day and night'. Within, it is not difficult to imagine the solitary existence of the penitent, 'The long mechanic pacings to and fro; the set grey life and apathetic end'. The interior has two 'floors', and the upper storey is divided into three compartments, the earliest of which are thought to have been hewn out around the mid-fourteenth century. The first compartment to be enetered is the chapel, which has a vaulted ceiling (or rather the rock is fashioned into the form of vaulting) and a traceried window which lights the second room, the sacristy. On a shield over the doorway to this are carved the emblems of the Passion. The third room is known as the solar, and below are two other rooms, a hall and a kitchen, all constructed round about the end of the fourteenth century.

About three miles north of Warkworth, the Aln, which we saw flowing through Hulne Park and past Alnwick Castle, reaches the sea. The small seaside resort of Alnmouth (the 'n' is sometimes shortened), on the north side of the estuary, with fine sands and an excellent golf course, has managed to remain exceptionally quiet and unspoilt. As the village has not been allowed to expand, it has retained the charm of simplicity and has escaped the evils that invariably attend those places that have been 'developed'. As viewed from the railway or the road from Warkworth, it presents an enticing picture, its long street of houses, with their red and grey roofs, running down to the end of a ridge thrust out between the estuary and the sea.

Alnmouth was probably that 'Twyford on the Alne', the scene in 684, according to Bede, of a great synod at which Cuthbert, then living as a hermit on the Farne Islands, was chosen to be Bishop of Lindisfarne. The present village was laid out in the twelfth century as a new 'borough' for the De Vescis of Alnwick. Charters for a market and for the collection of port tolls were granted in 1207 to Eustace de Vesci and were renewed by the Percys. The port began to decline when its harbour silted up in the sixteenth century, and the market has been lost, but the medieval town plan has survived. Life at Alnmouth revived in the eighteenth and early nineteenth centuries, when it enjoyed a considerable trade in corn and timber, among other things. The corn was stored in large granaries, curious high buildings with small windows, some of which still exist, though now converted into dwellings.

The stretch of coast northward from Alnmouth is one of the finest as well as one of the least known parts of the Northumbrian seaboard. The cliffs in general are not high, but they are broken up engagingly by little havens and rocky inlets known locally as 'churns', and here and there on the cliffs is a grassy cove where a small tent may conveniently be pitched. (It is an exhilarating experience to camp out along this coast and watch the sun rise out of the sea.) Boulmer is a small fishing village with a rock-bound haven and its row of houses facing away from the sea. Longhoughton (pronounced '-how-'), on a ridge 1½ miles inland, has a church, restored in 1873 (when the chancel was rebuilt), with a low, square tower, obviously meant for defence, and a nave and chancel arch that are all Norman work.

At Howick Haven is the mouth of a burn that flows through a secluded wooded dene, and on the cliffs to the north is the pleasant small village of Howick (the 'How' is pronounced as in 'now'). Howick Hall, in delightful gardens secreted among trees half a mile inland, was built in 1782 by William Newton and became the home of the second Earl Grey, promoter of the Reform Bill, who died in 1845. In the small church, built in 1746 but restored and Normanised in 1849, is a monument to the earl, by John Francis.

Howick is one of the few places where the coast can be approached by road. Cullernose Point, extending from the north side of its bay, is the first of several seaward outcrops of the Great Whin Sill, which ends in black basaltic cliffs some 120 feet high. The road makes a detour to reach the grey fishing village of Craster, with a small harbour, noted for its kippers, and with flowery gardens, a welcome sight, on the cliffs. Craster Tower, above the village, was mentioned in 1415 and has a wing added in 1769.

A path runs north along the low cliffs to Dunstanburgh Castle (pronounced '-bu-rur'), perhaps the most picturesque of the many strongholds in the Border and the most romantically situated, occupying the whole of the extensive summit of an isolated hill, an outcrop of the Great Whin Sill. The singular plateau, with an area amounting to about 11 acres, is protected on the north by a basalt cliff over 100 feet high, on the east by the jagged rocks of the sea-coast, and on the west by a natural precipice. Only on the south, where the slope is more gradual, is the site at all vulnerable, and there it is guarded by the magnificent gatehouse-keep and by the massive wall extending seaward to the Egyncleugh Tower, in addition to which the sea apparently came up to the foot of the slope in medieval times, forming a pool large enough to be used by the ships of the period.

The termination of the name, like that of Bamburgh, suggests a fortified settlement here in Anglian times. It seems highly probable that a site of such outstanding strength would attract the attention of settlers from across the North Sea. But the existing fortress was begun only in 1313, by Thomas, second Earl of Lancaster, the opponent of Edward II, and was intended chiefly as a refuge. Although by this time the motte-and-bailey castle, as originally constructed at Alnwick, Warkworth, Norham and elsewhere, had been superseded by more substantial strongholds, Dunstanburgh, oddly enough, reverted to the more elementary type of fortification, a mere accentuation of the natural conditions.

The castle did not escape the attentions of the Scots, and when it passed into the hands of John of Gaunt, appointed Lieutenant of the Marches in 1380, he sealed up the gatehouse and converted it into a keep. This splendid structure consists of two huge semicircular or drum towers flanking a vaulted entrance archway, the passage through which led, very unusually, directly into the Inner Ward of the castle (its most vulnerable part) and there seems little doubt that it was this fundamental weakness that decided John of Gaunt to block up the passage and provide a new gateway, to the north-west. The main structure of the keep rose three storeys above the ground, but the drum towers were extended two storeys higher, and from these projected square turrets that rose higher again. Above the second floor, only fragments of the towers and turrets remain, but it is these, more than anything else, that give the castle its rugged and romantic outline.

Apart from the gatehouse-keep, the most impressive survival is the turreted Lilburn Tower, built in about 1325 and guarding the contemporary postern gate towards the northern end of the wall, which ends abruptly at the edge of Gull Crag, the sheer cliffs here being considered no doubt more than sufficient defence. Near the seaward end is Rumbling Churn, where a column of the basalt has dropped out, leaving a hole through which the sea 'rumbles', throwing up a spout as high as the castle in rough weather. The vast Outer Ward was used mainly as a protection for sheep and cattle, which could be driven in from the neighbouring pastures on the warning of an enemy's approach.

From Craster the road turns inland again, by way of Dunstan, one of the claimants to be the birthplace of Duns Scotus, the medieval scholar and theologian. Others are Duns in Berwickshire and Down in Ulster, but the controversy seems never likely to be settled. The road goes north to Embleton, which can be reached also by a footpath across the sand-dunes from Dunstanburgh Castle. The village stands in a bleak position on the top of a ridge, away from the sea, but at the mercy of the harsh north-east winds. The much-restored church dates back to the thirteenth century, and parts of the original structure may be seen in the nave and the lower part of the tunnel-vaulted tower. The living of Embleton has been the gift of Merton College, Oxford, since its inception and the vicarage incorporates a tower built by the college for the priest between 1332 and 1341. Nearly two miles farther inland is Fallodon Hall, an eighteenth-century brick house, much rebuilt after a fire in 1917. It was the home of Viscount Grey of Fallodon, who carefully nurtured a bird-sanctuary here, but the birds unfortunately all disappeared soon after his death in 1935.

Northward from Embleton Bay, firm sands bounded by wide-spreading dunes stretch out, almost without interruption, as far as Seahouses and Bamburgh. This shore has an atmosphere more readily

sensed than described; the feeling of a subtle mystery and an elusive beauty depend on the changing relationship between the colours of sand, sea
and sky. When the sky is overcast, grey sea is separated from grey sand
only by the thin, straight line of foam, and desolation sits on the scene;
and when a 'haar' blows in from the sea, blotting out the landscape, the
sad booming of the unseen waves and the low wind among the coarse
grasses of the dunes is eerie in the extreme. But when the sun filters
through, the wide sands shine with an opalescent light, the sea is
transformed into a heaving deep-blue mass, and the scene has a loveliness
which of its kind is not easily matched elsewhere.

No other sea-coast in the country, save that of Norfolk, welcomes a
bird population at once as rich and as varied. The Northumberland coast
is the first landing place for those birds migrating from Scandinavia to the
Mediterranean in the autumn, and it sees them again on their return
passage in the spring. Not only the Farne Islands, now an official bird-
sanctuary, but the sandy wastes of Holy Island and the long extent of the
flat shore as far as the Tweed afford protection to the birds during the
breeding season and while they prepare for their journey over the North
Sea. Of the 400 species on the list for the whole of Britain, as many as
260 can be seen on this coast, either as residents, summer visitors or
winter migrants; this apart from rare and accidental visitors.

Embleton Bay is succeeded, going northward, by St Mary's or Newton Haven, the curiously named Football Hole, and the long Beadnell
Bay. At the north end of this is the fishing village and quiet summer resort
of Beadnell, with a fine sandy beach and a small harbour overlooked by
disused eighteenth-century lime-kilns. Seahouses, farther north, is a larger
fishing community that has expanded to become quite a popular seaside
resort, and its busy harbour is the point of embarkation for the Farne
Islands.

The Farne Islands are a widely-scattered archipelago of small islands
and rocks, lying between $1\frac{1}{2}$ and $4\frac{3}{4}$ miles off the coast and forming the
easternmost extremity of the Great Whin Sill. There are about 30
altogether, but the number visible varies from 15 upward, depending on
the state of the tide, as some rocks can be seen only at low water, while
others never appear above the surface at any time. The islands are
separated into two groups by Staple Sound, a channel three-quarters of a
mile wide between the nearest points. The chief island in the nearer group

is the Inner Farne, the largest of the whole series and the nearest to the mainland, with an area at low water of about 16 acres, though 11 of these consist almost wholly of bare rock. Some parts of the larger islands are covered by a peaty soil, which grows the characteristic seaside plants, but there are no trees, the only woody vegetation being the remnants of a few elders planted many years ago on the Inner Farne.

The sheer basaltic rocks of which the islands are composed show at their most impressive in the cliffs, 80 feet high, on the south and west sides of the Inner Farne and also at the south-west extremity of Staple Island, the largest of the outer group, where three huge columnar stacks, about 60 feet high, known as the Pinnacles, have been weathered away from the island. Many of the islands are deeply fissured, and in The Churn, on the Inner Farne, the sea sometimes projects a column of water up to 90 feet high.

Other islands of the outer group are the Brownsman, on which bird-watchers are maintained (as well as on the Inner Farne) during the breeding season, and Longstone, the farthest out apart from the small rocks of the Knavestone. The lighthouse on Longstone occupies the site of that from which Grace Darling, in the early hours of the wild morning of 7 September 1838, set out in a small boat with her aged father, the lighthouse-keeper, to rescue the survivors of the *Forfarshire*, a ship of 400 tons bound from Hull to Dundee that had gone aground on the dangerous rocks of the Big Harcar.

The first visitor to the Farnes of whom there is any record was St Aidan, Bishop of Lindisfarne from 635 to 651, who often withdrew here for meditation. But the islands first owed their fame to St Cuthbert, who in 676, when Prior of Lindisfarne, retired to the Inner Farne, where he built with his own hands a rough hermitage of stones and turf. Here he lived alone until 684, when he was persuaded to accept, reluctantly, the Bishopric of Lindisfarne, a position which he held for only two years. He resigned to seek again the solitude of the Inner Farne, but he died here, as a result of the austere existence he had imposed upon himself, only three months after his return.

On the Inner Farne is a tower built in about 1500 by Prior Castell of Durham, on the site of Cuthbert's hermitage, and used for the first warning-light on the Farnes in 1673. The chapel on the island was rebuilt in 1370, but was restored in 1848 by Archdeacon Thorp, who brought the oak stalls and other fine woodwork of the time of Bishop Cosin (1660–72) from Durham Cathedral. The views from the Inner Farne over the cliffs of the other islands and towards Bamburgh are superb.

The islands were bought in 1924 for the National Trust and are administered by a committee composed of representatives of the Trust and the Farne Islands Association, a body formed after the passing of the first Bird Protection Act, in 1880, to watch over the many birds that visited the islands annually to breed. Among the wealth of sea and shore birds which now breed here must be mentioned the eider duck, the cormorant, the shag, the fulmar, the oyster-catcher, the ringed plover, the guillemot, the razor-bill and the puffin, as well as several species of tern and gull. The eider duck, known locally as 'St Cuthbert's chicken' because of the interest taken in it by that recluse, breeds regularly on the Farnes and is protected by law throughout the year. It is best seen in late May and early June, when as many as 300 nests are to be found on the Inner Farne, apart from those on Staple Island, Brownsman, Longstone and other islands.

The Farnes are the only breeding place on the east coast of Britain of the Atlantic seal, or grey seal, as it is more familiarly known, though variations of black and white colouring are not uncommon. Its favourite haunt is the Megstone, the chief of a small outlying group of islands to the west.

As the Farne Islands are a bird sanctuary, only the Inner Farne and Staple Island are normally accessible to visitors, and then only from the beginning of April to the end of September. Landing tickets are obtainable before sailing from the Information Centre at Seahouses harbour or on going ashore from the watchers appointed by the National Trust. Access is further restricted during the breeding season, which lasts from mid-May to mid-July. Permits for landing then and permission to land from October to March must be obtained from the National Trust Warden at Seahouses (telephone 066 572 651).

CHAPTER NINE

Bamburgh and Holy Island

Continuing northward along the coast from Seahouses (Chapter 8), we skirt the broad St Aidan's Dunes, which belong to the National Trust; from their tops we have a fine view of the Farne Islands. Before us we have a magnificent prospect of the great stronghold of Bamburgh (pronounced '-bu-rur'), poised high on its huge, precipitous rock like some romantic castle of childhood's dreams or medieval legend. No place in Britain is better fitted to stimulate the imagination than Bamburgh, the royal city of the Saxon Bernicia and the capital of united Northumbria when it extended from the Humber to the Firth of Forth. 'At Bamburgh, above all, we feel that we are pilgrims come to do our service at one of the great cradles of our national life', and 'round Bamburgh and its founder, Ida, all Northumbrian history gathers.'

The castle enjoys an outstanding position on the summit of an immense basaltic rock, part of the Great Whin Sill which extends out to the Farnes. The rock is a quarter of a mile long and upwards of 150 feet high, precipitous on every side except that facing the sea, and this came right up to the foot of the rock until wind and storm began to throw up the white sand-dunes.

Excavations have shown that the top of the rock was occupied in prehistoric and Roman times, and Bamburgh has been claimed (somewhat doubtfully) as the 'Joyous Gard' of Sir Galahad in the Arthurian legends. The fortified city was founded in 547, according to the *Anglo-Saxon Chronicle*, by King Ida, known as the 'flame-bearer', and it became from the outset the capital of the kings of Northumbria. Ethelfrith the Destroyer (Ida's grandson), who died in 617, reigned here for 12 years, then gave the castle to his wife, Bebba, from whom (according to Bede) it took its name of Bebbanburh, and subsequently Bamburgh. The seat of government was removed in the mid-8th century to Corbridge, on the Tyne, and later to York, but Bamburgh continued to be the residence of the monarchy.

During the course of its long and stormy history, Bamburgh was besieged many times. In 651 it was attacked by Penda, the pagan king of the Mercians, who attempted, unsuccessfully, to destroy it by fire; and in 705 it sustained a siege by Eadwulf, who had seized the throne of Northumbria on the death of Aldfrith. In 774 the Northumbrian king Alcred fled here on being driven from York. At this time Bamburgh was described by the chronicler Simeon of Durham as 'although not large, (it) is a very strongly fortified town'. Bamburgh seems to have escaped the Vikings who harried Lindisfarne in 875, but it was stormed and pillaged three times between 933 and 1015. After the appalling devastation of the North by William the Conqueror, Bamburgh remained the only inhabited town in the whole of Northumberland; and in 1095, during the revolt of Robert de Mowbray, it withstood a siege by William Rufus, who attempted to blockade the stronghold by erecting against the wall a wooden fort which he called 'Malvoisin', or evil neighbour. During the Wars of the Roses the castle was largely in the hands of the Yorkists, though the unfortunate Henry VI made it his residence for more than a year before the decisive Battle of Hexham in 1463.

The fortress extends over the whole of the upper surface of its great crag. The Saxon royal palace was situated at the eastern end of the plateau, while the remaining (and larger) area was covered by the city. The Norman stronghold followed this arrangement in having the keep, with the chapel and domestic buildings, at the eastward end, while the remainder consisted of two large wards or baileys which were little more than enclosures for the garrison and for prisoners. The original entrance was at the western end, and ruins of a postern, protected by a barbican, can still be seen here. Later, an entrance was constructed by the Normans at the opposite end, consisting of a gateway between two semicircular towers, with a projecting barbican that has since disappeared, the whole set well below the level of the summit plateau.

Beyond the eastern gatehouse, a passage through an inner gateway ascends towards the top of the rock, an arrangement perhaps unparalleled, except at Edinburgh Castle, where too the passage was assailable from the rock summit, as well as from a wall bounding it on the outer side. An attacker would have to force his way through two gateways and up the long sunken passage, where he could be assaulted from above and at the side, and even then, supposing these difficulties to be overcome, would find himself only in the central bailey, or East Ward, as it was called, and at a point where this was overlooked by the great keep. To gain the inmost ward and attack the main body of the castle, he would have to force yet a third gateway. The difficulty of effecting an entrance, combined with the practical impossibility of scaling the precipices which guarded the castle on the inland side or of attacking it from the sea, rendered the stronghold well-nigh impregnable, given an adequate garrison.

The massive keep, which is the largest in the Border with the exception of that at Norham, was built in about 1164 by Henry II, who was responsible for so many fine keeps. The entrance is unusual in being on the ground floor, instead of over a forebuilding (as can still be seen at Newcastle and Carlisle); presumably a strongly guarded entrance was considered unnecessary.

After the disturbances of the Middle Ages were at an end, the castle passed into the hands of the Forsters, but they so misused their splendid inheritance by reckless extravagance that their estates were ordered to be sold to defray their debts. The castle was purchased by Lord Crewe, Bishop of Durham, in 1704, and on his death his trustees, and in particular Dr John Sharp, Archdeacon of Lindisfarne, undertook an extensive 'restoration', at the same time pioneering a social welfare scheme that lasted until the late nineteenth century. The long range of buildings on the south side of the East Ward that creates such an imposing effect as one looks up from the village is entirely the work of Dr Sharp (carried out between 1758 and 1792) and he also very probably made sundry alterations to the keep. In 1894 the castle was bought by the first Lord Armstrong, the engineer (who died in 1900), and he began a second, and even more expensive restoration, which took 30 years to complete. These restored state apartments now contain a miscellaneous collection of relics, mostly gathered by Lord Armstrong.

Bamburgh village, dominated by the castle, is quiet and colourful, and happily it is entirely unspoilt. The single street, with its row of grey stone cottages set back behind a wooded green, mounts easily from the base of the castle rock, which shelters it from the wind off the sea. At the upper end of the village is the church, one of the finest in the Border; the interior, in particular, is extraordinarily spacious and beautiful. A church, of wood, was first built here some time after 635 for St Aidan, who died in a cell attached to the west end of it in 651. The present church is almost entirely in the Early English style of the thirteenth century; the long chancel, the most pleasing in Northumberland, was built when the church became the property of the Augustinian canons of Nostell Priory in Yorkshire. Below the chancel is an unusual vaulted crypt, rediscovered in 1837, when it was found to contain the coffins of several members of the Forster family, including the famous Dorothy, who died in 1739; her uncle Ferdinando, shot in the streets of Newcastle in 1701 by Sir John Fenwick; and her brother, General Thomas Forster, who was condemned to death for his part in the Jacobite revolt of 1715, and whose rescue from prison by his intrepid sister is recounted in Sir Walter Besant's romance of *Dorothy Forster*. He died in France in 1738 and his body was brought back to Bamburgh.

In the churchyard is the tomb of Grace Darling, an ornate Gothic affair with a canopy, quite out of keeping with the simplicity of that heroine. Grace was born in a cottage nearly opposite in 1815 and died of tuberculosis in a house beside the green in 1842, just short of her twenty-seventh birthday. A memorial museum near her birthplace contains not only reminders of the Darling family and the ill-fated *Forfarshire*, but the boat in which the rescue was made, a coble, 21 feet long and 6 feet broad, of a design that is typical, with its high prow and double keel, of the boats still used by the fishermen of this coast.

Beyond Bamburgh we reach Budle Bay (pronounced 'Bew-'), an almost land-locked estuary from which the sea recedes at low tide, leaving a great expanse of sand and mud flats. It is difficult to realise that here was once a port of some importance, given a charter in the thirteenth century by Henry III. To the south of Waren Mill is the outcrop of Spindlestone Heugh (pronounced 'heuff', as usual), scene of the ballad of the 'Laidley Worm', or loathsome serpent. On the north side of Budle Bay are the wastes of Ross Links and beyond these the castle of Holy Island can be seen, standing fairy-like on its pinnacle of rock.

The road from Budle Bay runs inland to reach the Great North Road short of Belford, the only place of any size on the 29 miles between

Alnwick and Berwick. An old market town situated on the slope of a hill, its appearance, as approached from the south, with the Blue Bell inn at the head of the street, is distinctly pleasing, and it has a fine Hall built in 1756 by James Paine. During medieval times Belford was unfortunate in being often in the path of the harrying Scots, and even as late as 1639 it was described as 'the most miserable, beggarly town', and its houses were mere hovels, roofed only with heather and sods. Its revival came with the development of coach travel in the eighteenth century.

The Berwick road runs between the wooded Kyloe Hills (Chapter 7) and the great bay off which lies Holy Island, the approach to which starts from the inn at West Mains. We cross the main Newcastle-Edinburgh railway at the station of Beal and from the hamlet of that name descend to the shore.

If any place can justifiably claim to be the birthplace of Christianity in the North of England, it is certainly Holy Island, or Lindisfarne, as it was anciently called. When the Christian religion was re-established in Northumbria (after the pagan reaction following the mission of Paulinus) on what proved to be an enduring basis, its seat was the church of Lindisfarne, from which it spread, first through the kingdom, then subsequently throughout the whole of the North.

This historical fact alone would render Holy Island worthy as the goal of a pilgrimage, but when we consider also the singular setting of this cradle of Northern Christianity, then history is fortified by romance and the pilgrimage becomes doubly interesting. Lindisfarne earns the name of island only at high tide, when the sands connecting it with the mainland are covered and it is completely cut off, except by boat. But as the water recedes, the broad expanse of sand is exposed and it is then absolutely safe to cross.

> *For with the flow and ebb, its style*
> *Varies from continent to isle;*
> *Dry-shod o'er sands, twice every day,*
> *The pilgrims to the shrine find way:*
> *Twice every day, the waves efface*
> *Of staves and sandall'd feet the trace.*

The modern pilgrim now crosses the sands by a causeway, constructed in 1955, but the journey can be made only within a period of between 2 hours before low water and 3½ hours after. It is possible to walk across the sands, but these are never wholly dry and in one place a considerable stream has to be forded. The old carriage route (about 2¾ miles) took a direct course towards the village of Holy Island, passing a series of 'refuges', mounted high above the water on poles, that must have witnessed many a humorous and occasionally a tragic event, when travellers were cut off by the tide. The causeway makes a shorter crossing (of about a mile) towards the northern end of the island, then runs in the lee of the Snook, a great waste of sandhills flung out westward from the main body of the island and now a nature reserve. Coming ashore, the road enters the north end of the grey village, which for most of the year is a bleak and windswept place, though it is very popular during the summer holiday period.

The history of Holy Island begins in 634, when St Aidan, accepting the invitation of King Oswald, arrived from Iona, off the west coast of Scotland, to teach Christianity to the Northumbrians. In his choice of this site he was probably influenced by three considerations: its insularity, securely cut off from the mainland when the tide was in; its similarity in some respects to the island he had left; and its comforting proximity to the royal palace at Bamburgh. Here, on this lonely island, assisted by the enthusiastic king, Aidan created the first diocese in the North of England and also founded a monastery, himself combining the offices of bishop and abbot. After his death in 651, he was succeeded by two more Celtic monks, Finan (who baptized the pagan kings of Mercia and East Anglia) and Colman, who on his defeat at the Synod of Whitby in 664 by Wilfrid (the Romaniser, as he has been aptly styled), returned again to Iona. The next bishop, Tuda, subjected himself to the Roman discipline, but died within a year of his appointment and was followed by Wilfrid himself, who then transferred the seat of the bishopric from Lindisfarne to York. As the result of a quarrel between Wilfrid and the Archbishop of Canterbury, however, the diocese was divided, and Eata, a disciple of Aidan and already Abbot of Lindisfarne, was in 678 appointed the fifth bishop here. His successor was the most renowned of Northumbrian churchmen and one of the outstanding figures of ecclesiastical history – St Cuthbert.

First heard of as a shepherd boy on the Lammermuirs, Cuthbert became a monk at the abbey of Mailros (Old Melrose), on the Tweed, soon attracting the attention of Eata, the first abbot there. He accompanied Eata to the new monastery which had been founded at Ripon, but on the installation of Wilfrid as Abbot of Ripon, he returned as prior to Mailros, from which he wandered throughout the south of Scotland, gaining a reputation as an eloquent and persuasive preacher. When Eata was promoted abbot at Lindisfarne in 664, he elected Cuthbert to the position of prior here. But in 676 a distaste for the pomp and circumstance that had grown round the monastic life, combined with his essential humility and that desire for self-mortification not uncommon among early martyrs, decided Cuthbert to retreat to the Inner Farne. After his death in 687 on his return to that island, as already recounted, his body was brought back to Lindisfarne and buried in the place of honour on the right-hand side of the high altar.

Lindisfarne was the scene of the first attack by the Vikings on the English coast, in 793, when they pillaged the monastery and murdered most of the monks. When the Vikings descended on the island again in 875 the monks hurriedly disinterred the body of St Cuthbert and escaped with it to the mainland. For over seven years, bearing the saint's coffin, they wandered uneasily from place to place, eventually resting at Chester-le-Street, where the see was established for 113 years before its removal to Durham, which can thus claim to be the direct successor of the original diocese of Lindisfarne. For over two centuries after its destruction by the Vikings, the abbey lay deserted, but shortly after 1081 Benedictines from Durham founded a priory here, and it is to this establishment that the existing remains belong.

Except for a few carved stones in the priory museum, nothing survives of the great cathedral-monastery. But its place in the history of English culture is assured by two masterpieces now in the British Museum (the Lindisfarne Gospels, an illuminated manuscript of about A.D. 700, and the *Liber Vitae*, with characters drawn in gold and silver) and by the wooden coffin of St Cuthbert and its contents, now in the Cathedral Library at Durham.

Lindisfarne Priory, mostly built of a warm red sandstone very pleasing to the eye, is the most picturesque of the monastic buildings in Northumberland and it has been glowingly described by Scott in *Mar-*

mion. The ruins include an admirable example of a Benedictine church of the late eleventh century, bearing a very strong resemblance not only to the great mother-church of Durham, but also to the sister churches of Selby and Dunfermline. The west doorway of the church is a noble example of Norman workmanship, with a rich zigzag-moulded arch. Of the nave, only two bays of the north arcade have survived complete, but it is here, more than anywhere, that the striking resemblance to the cathedral at Durham is most evident; the easternmost pier is cylindrical and carved with a delicate chevron pattern, while the next pier is composed of clustered shafts, an arrangement followed exactly at Durham. Of the central tower only a single graceful rib remains, known as the 'rainbow arch,' but this is enriched with zigzag ornament, like a similar arch in Durham Cathedral.

The most extensive remains are those of the transepts, each with an apsidal chapel, and the choir, which previously ended in an apse (its foundations have been laid bare). This was lengthened and altered to a square end in about 1140, and the Perpendicular window is a late fourteenth-century insertion. The most significant feature of the domestic buildings, which are mostly of the thirteenth and fourteenth centuries, is their defensive character. At the east end they were protected by a tower (the base still exists) that may have served as a keep, and on the south side are the ruins of a gatehouse, with both outer and inner doorways, by which the cloister was entered from an outer courtyard. This last was further protected, on the west, by a second gatehouse and barbican, of the type still to be seen at Tynemouth Priory.

Near the priory ruins is the parish church of Holy Island, which, because of the proximity and the greater historical and romantic interest of the priory, can easily be overlooked. The Norman north arcade was partly built in the late twelfth century and its stout piers, with their alternate courses of red and white stones, are the most striking feature of the interior. The arcade was extended westward in about 1300, when also the south arcade was built, and the long chancel, characteristic of Northumbrian churches, was rebuilt in the late thirteenth century. At the west end of the church is a massive arched buttress, part of the work of about 1300, which is carried up to support a typical Northumbrian bellcote, rebuilt or added in the eighteenth century. In the churchyard is a statue of St Aidan, 9 feet high, carved in 1958 by Kate Parbury.

The fishing harbour of Holy Island is sheltered to some extent by the long rib of basaltic rock that rises at the south-east end of the island and forms the northernmost extremity of the Great Whin Sill. At its seaward end, this rib is forced up into the high steep-sided pyramid of Beblowe Crag, and on this is mounted the small Lindisfarne Castle, towering up like a lesser edition of Bamburgh Castle. The castle was built in about 1550, at a time when all harbours had to be 'fensed with bulwarks and blockehouses against the Scots', but it was never tested, and after the Union of the Crowns it lost its significance, though a garrison was maintained until the nineteenth century. The ruins were bought in 1902 by Edward Hudson, the founder of *Country Life*, for whom Edwin Lutyens created a romantic private dwelling, with vaulted rooms that give the impression of being hewn out of the solid rock. Among Hudson's many famous visitors here were Lytton Strachey, the historian, who didn't like the castle (it was 'very dark, with nowhere to sit, and nothing but stone under, over and round you'), Madame Suggia, the 'cellist, Lord Asquith, the Liberal Prime Minister, and Lord Baden-Powell, founder of the Boy Scouts. The castle was given to the National Trust in 1944. From the high plateau of its top fine views extend inland to the Cheviots and along the coast in both directions: to Bamburgh Castle and the Farne Islands, and northward to Berwick at the mouth of the Tweed.

CHAPTER TEN

Berwick and the Lower Tweed

Considered from a purely geographical point of view, crossing the Tweed to Berwick (pronounced 'Ber-rik') ought to take one from England into Scotland. But though it is situated on the north bank of the river, and is therefore geographically in Scotland, the town is included in the county of Northumberland, an entirely anomalous position whichever way it is considered, for Berwick bears the characteristics of a Scottish town rather than an English one, in culture and commerce it looks more to Scotland than to England, the Scottish accent predominates here, and it is divorced from the Scottish shire that still bears its name. For a long time the town held an even more anomalous position, being administratively in England but enjoying to some extent the rights of a 'free town', with 'liberties' extending for nearly 4 miles up the Tweed and over 3 miles northward along the coast.

Berwick is crowded on to a long outlying bastion thrown down by the grey, bare Lammermuir Hills and turning the Tweed southward in the last mile of its course to the sea. The older part of the town faces away from the sea, clinging to the western flank of this promontory and overlooking the river, a factor which contributed greatly to its military strength in the uncertain times of the Middle Ages. As seen from the railway approaching the Royal Border Bridge on the south, the clustered assembly of red-tiled roofs, with the imposing steeple of the Town Hall rising from their midst, and the grey ramparts of the protecting walls topped by green mounds and set off by the shining estuary of the Tweed, make Berwick the most appealing of Border towns. This impression is accentuated when exploring its steep, cobbled streets, looking into narrow entries and alleyways, and traversing its unique walls. Though the town has many fine Georgian houses, no medieval houses have survived, these having all been destroyed in the long series of sieges to which Berwick was subjected. But the town retains its medieval street plan and the streets themselves still manage to express to some extent the stirring atmosphere of the Middle Ages.

For well over 300 years, Berwick suffered from its unfortunate position on the frontier, a 'shuttlecock between the contending nations'. The town changed hands no fewer than 13 times between 1147, when it was surrendered by William the Lion after his capture at the Battle of Alnwick, and 1482, when it was finally taken for England by Richard, Duke of Gloucester, later Richard III. Under a treaty signed by Edward VI and Mary, Queen of Scots, Berwick was created a 'free burgh', an extra-territorial community with a government of its own, and it retained this independent status until the Reform Act of 1885, all Acts of Parliament and other statutes containing the special reference 'and to our town of Berwick-upon-Tweed'.

The castle, which stood high above the Tweed, was built in about 1167 by Henry II, but the only surviving part is the west wall, which forms the boundary of the railway station yard. Much of the castle was demolished in 1847 to make way for the station, over which Robert Stephenson the engineer inscribed, appropriately, 'The final act of union'. The platforms are thought to occupy the site of the Great Hall, from which Edward I in 1292 pronounced his fateful decision in favour of John Baliol, who was in dispute with Robert Bruce for the crown of Scotland. Four years later the successful disputant threw off his allegiance to the English king and attempted to hold Berwick, but Edward captured and ransacked the town. It was this action, more than any other, that sowed the seeds of distrust and strife that lasted until the Union of the Crowns. Edward ordered that strong walls be built to protect the town. These, though altered later, survive on the west and south sides, facing the river and its estuary, but the most noticeable survival is the flanking wall descending steeply from the site of the castle to the river, just west of the railway bridge, with the water tower near its foot. Of the walls on the north side only earthworks now exist (or earth-covered masonry), except for the lower part of the octagonal Bell Tower (heightened in Elizabethan times).

The new walls did not succeed in keeping out the Scots; first William Wallace and then Robert Bruce (grandson of Baliol's opponent) gained an entry to the town. But in 1305 Wallace was betrayed and captured, and after his execution one of his quarters was set up on or near the bridge. In the following year the Countess of Buchan, for her offence in crowning Robert Bruce as King of Scotland (a privilege she claimed as a daughter of the house of Fife, which had exercised that right since the reign of Malcolm Canmore), was confined in a cage within the castle, an imprisonment that lasted for six years. The castle was retaken by Robert Bruce in 1318, but ten years later his son David (afterwards David II) was married in Berwick to the sister of Edward III in an attempt to enforce a lasting peace.

At this time Berwick was a royal burgh and one of the most important commercial centres in Scotland. It was described, not wholly fancifully, as the 'Alexandria of the North'; it 'took rank with Ghent, Rotterdam and other great cities of the Low Countries, and was almost the rival of London in mercantile enterprise'. But in 1333 Edward III attempted to retake the town, and as an inducement to the governor, Sir Alexander Seton, to surrender, hanged Seton's son, whom he held as hostage, within sight of the walls. Though this ruse failed to influence the Scots, they were obliged by lack of supplies and the non-arrival of reinforcements to withdraw from the protection of the walls and castle and to encounter the English on Halidon Hill, the prominent ridge rising behind the town. While the king himself attacked Berwick, the main body of the English army under Sir William Montagu was massed on the top of the hill to await the Scots. By the advantage of their superior position and the weight of their formidable bowmen, later to make themselves famous at Crécy and Poitiers, the English were enabled to inflict a crushing defeat on the Scots, thus reversing the decision at Bannockburn 19 years earlier. After this calamity Berwick was surrendered by the Scots and never regained its former prestige.

In 1461 the town was relinquished by Henry VI, then a refugee in Scotland, but in 1482 it was regained, for the last time, by Richard 'Crookback' for his brother Edward IV. Henceforth Berwick was organised as a bastion of the English defences against the Scots, a position it held until the Union in 1603. Henry VIII decided to make improvements to the walls to accommodate more artillery; two gun towers were added to the flanking wall of the castle (one at the riverside end) and a much larger tower, about 100 feet in diameter, known as Lord's Mount, was built at the north-east angle of the defences. During the reign of Edward VI a large square citadel was begun, extending through the wall on the east side, but this was abandoned by January 1558, when Mary Tudor ordered Sir Richard Lee, an eminent military engineer, to design a completely new system of fortifications. Mary died in November of that year, but the work was pushed forward at the instigation of the new queen, Elizabeth I.

The Elizabethan Ramparts, as they are usually called, are unique in Britain, but they were based on an Italian model already tried out at Verona (in 1523) and Antwerp (1545). The third of their type to be built, the walls of Berwick are today the most important example in Europe. They consist of curtain walls, 20 feet high, on the north and east of the town, with a bastion in the centre of each wall, the Cumberland Bastion (the most complete) on the north and the Windmill Bastion on the east; a corner bastion, the Brass Bastion (altered after 1564), on the north-east; and two half-bastions, Meg's Mount at the north-west end of the wall, and King's Mount at the south-east end. On the east side the new wall followed the line of the Edwardian wall, which by this time was either in a state of disrepair or, more likely, considered inadequate against artillery. On the north the Elizabethan wall was built about a quarter of a mile south of the medieval wall, so that the castle was excluded from the new defences. It was intended to extend the wall round the south and west sides of the town, but this was never proceeded with and the Edwardian walls were repaired instead.

The bastions were in effect a development of the medieval flanking tower, square or semicircular in plan (such as can be seen at the castles of Alnwick and Warkworth). They consist of massive projections from the line of the wall, each having two flanking faces, at right angles to the wall, and two outer faces. The flanking faces have each a deep recess to conceal the gun emplacements, while the outer faces are arranged, not parallel to the walls, but at a salient angle to them, i.e. extending slightly outward from their ends, so that every part of the ramparts could be raked by concealed guns, thus rendering the whole of the defences unassailable. The walls and bastions were completely surrounded by an outer ditch about 150 feet wide. On the top of the walls are earthen mounds,

16 feet high, which were raised in 1639–53, with gun platforms on all
the bastions (except King's Mount) to give a more advantageous range of
fire. Little remains of an outflanking wall extending north from the Brass
Bastion to Lord's Mount.

Four gates penetrated the Elizabethan Ramparts, but the Cowport,
leading to the pastures outside the town towards the cliffs, is the only one
to have survived intact. The Scots Gate, by which the Great North Road
enters the town from the direction of Scotland, was reconstructed and
widened in 1815; the Bridge Gate, leading to the old bridge across the
river, was removed in 1825; the Shore Gate, providing access to the
quay, was rebuilt in the eighteenth century. The Ness Gate, giving access
to the estuary of the Tweed and the then new pier, was cut through only
in 1816.

The complete circuit of the walls can be walked, and it is well worth
making, not only for the historic interest but for the succession of intimate
views that it opens up of the town, the river and the bridges, as well as for
the wider views of the coast and the spacious countryside around.

Three bridges span the Tweed at Berwick. The oldest is the rugged
stone bridge of 15 irregular arches, stoutly buttressed, built in 1613–20
by order of James VI of Scotland, who, it is said, found the previous
bridge unstable when he passed over it on his way to assume the English
crown as James I. Close by is the incongruous Royal Tweed Bridge, a
utilitarian ferro-concrete structure completed in 1928, by which the Great
North Road enters the town from the south. Its main span of $361\frac{1}{2}$ feet
was the largest in Britain when it was built. Farther upstream is the Royal
Border Bridge, 2,000 feet long, which carries the London-Edinburgh
railway across the river on 28 tall arches. Designed by Robert Stephenson
and opened in 1847, it is the most imposing of the Tweed bridges, standing at its greatest height nearly 130 feet above the river-bed.

From the old bridge we could follow the line of the Edwardian walls
southward by Quay Walls, facing the river and bordered by good
eighteenth century houses, including the Custom House (No. 18), of
about 1800. Several of the houses were well restored in 1975 in
collaboration with the National Trust and the Berwick-upon-Tweed
Town Preservation Trust. From the Shore Gate, Sandgate and its con-
tinuation, the broad Hide Hill, climb steeply to the King's Arms Hotel,
where Dickens stayed in 1858 and again in 1861, while on his famous

lecture tours. Marygate, the broad once-cobbled main street, still serves as a market place on Wednesdays and Saturdays, and the annual May Fair is also held here. At the foot of the street rises the Town Hall, with an impressive portico dominated by a tower and tall spire. Built in 1754–60, it was designed by S. and J. Worrell, though Joseph Dodds, the builder, inscribed his name as architect on the portico.

Church Street goes on north from the Town Hall towards the classical Parish Church, secreted in an angle of the walls and almost hidden by trees. One of only four churches built during the Commonwealth, it was designed in 1648 by Edward Carter for Colonel George Fenwick, the Puritan governor of Berwick, and completed in 1652, though the curious corner turrets and the chancel are nineteenth-century additions. Facing the church are the Ravensdowne Barracks, the headquarters from 1881 to 1964 of the King's Own Scottish Borderers and still containing the regimental museum. Built in 1717–21, the design has been attributed to Sir John Vanbrugh, the architect of Blenheim Palace and Castle Howard, as well as of Seaton Delaval Hall (in Northumberland). Splendidly carved over the gateway are the arms of George I.

Berwick has a fishing fleet and a boatbuilding yard (established in 1751 and re-opened in the early 1950s) and is noted for its 'cockles', not shellfish but a striped peppermint sweetmeat. Tweedmouth, on the other side of the river and mainly an industrial quarter, is extended to the south-east by the quiet seaside resort of Spittal, which has a good sandy beach and is an excellent place for watching the migrating birds.

From a point nearly 4 miles above Berwick Bridge, the Tweed forms for a distance of about 18 miles the Border between England and Scotland. It is at once the most beautiful and the most characteristic of Border rivers, in its lower course flowing through fertile country, known on the Scottish side as the Merse (from 'march', a boundary or frontier region), with many exquisite reaches skirted now by green, level meadows, now by steep, wooded banks. The Tweed is justly famous for its salmon fishing, and a ceremony of Blessing the Nets takes place at Norham, near midnight, on or near 14 February, to open the season.

Roads run from Berwick on both sides of the Tweed, but at some distance from river, so neither road gives the best impression of the deep-set waters. For those with leisure the Tweed is much better explored by way of the bankside footpath starting from Tweedmouth. The path passes opposite the wooded grounds of Paxton House to reach the Union Bridge (better known as the Chain Bridge), which crosses the river to Scotland. Built in 1820 by Captain Samuel Brown, using the wrought-iron link which he had patented in 1817, it is the earliest suspension bridge in Britain. The path skirts one of the finest bends of the Tweed below Horncliffe, an attractive village of red sandstone houses high up on a cliff above the river. From the mouth of the pretty Horncliffe Glen, a path goes across fields to the pink sandstone ruins of Norham Castle.

Norham Castle (pronounced 'Nor-ram'), the inspiration for several glowing landscapes by Turner, is one of the most imposing in addition to having been among the most important of Border strongholds. Situated on the top of a wood-enclosed rise that commands one of the few practicable fords across the lower part of the Tweed, it is guarded on its east side by a deep natural ravine and on its south and west sides by an artificial moat through which runs the road from Horncliffe.

The castle had an origin different from that of any other Border fortress; it was not a royal castle like Bamburgh or Carlisle, a noble fortified dwelling like Alnwick or Warkworth, or a place of retreat like Dunstanburgh, but an outpost of the powerful prince-bishops of Durham, who as counts-palatine exercised in their principality the rights and privileges that the sovereign enjoyed in the rest of the kingdom. Norham was from early times the capital of a district known as Norhamshire, which (like Islandshire, of which Lindisfarne was the capital) was detached from the county of Northumberland and formed part of the County Palatine of Durham, an arrangement that persisted until 1559, when these districts were alienated from the see of Durham and were vested in the Crown.

The castle, begun in 1121 by Bishop Ranulph Flambard, was probably of the usual motte-and-bailey type. From its bold position on the frontier, facing directly into Scotland, Norham had to withstand the first onslaught of many a Scottish invasion, and as early as 1136 it had already changed hands, being taken by David I during his incursion into Northumberland. Though the castle remained mostly in the possession of the bishops of Durham, it was requisitioned by the Crown and a royal garrison installed on more than one occasion when the loyalty of the bishop was in doubt.

The ground plan of the castle is in the shape of a quadrant or quarter-circle. The inner ward, together with the keep, forming the apex of the quadrant, is separated from the outer ward by a deep moat (now dry). The keep, the gates and the walls of the castle were all completed before 1174 by Richard de Wolviston, a master-mason from Durham, for Bishop Hugh Pudsey or de Puiset. The keep, the largest in the Border and one of the most impressive in Britain, was formerly three storeys high and had steep-pitched roofs, above the line of which the walls were extended. Often besieged and battered, and as often repaired or rebuilt, it now exhibits work of every century from the twelfth to the sixteenth.

In 1209 King John concluded with William the Lion here one of the many treaties between their countries, but five years later Alexander II besieged the castle for 40 days, though without success. Edward I was entertained here in 1291 by the ambitious Antony Bek, and in the following year Baliol paid homage to the king in the Great Hall. In 1318 Robert Bruce laid siege to the castle for nearly a year, using the latest artillery, but to no avail, and in the following year he besieged it again for seven months, with equal lack of success. During the Wars of the Roses, Norham was alternately in the hands of the Lancastrians and the Yorkists. It was refortified by Bishop Fox in 1494 against Scottish invasion, and in 1497 it successfully withstood a siege by James IV when he crossed the Tweed in support of the pretender, Perkin Warbeck. But in 1513 the Scottish king crossed the Border again, assaulting and partly wrecking the castle on his way to the fateful field of Flodden. A vivid impression of the stronghold before the battle is given by Scott in the opening lines of *Marmion*. After the defeat of the Scots at Flodden the castle was again repaired and was then declared to be 'unprignable', but from 1550 it was allowed to fall into disuse and in 1559 it passed out of the hands of the prince-bishops of Durham.

The village of Norham, one of the pleasantest in the Border, is charmingly situated on the bank of the gracious Tweed, with the 'mouldering pile' of the castle rising out of the trees beyond the head of its long, irregular street of grey cottages, which line each side of a spacious green. To the first church here, built by Ecfrith, Bishop of Lindisfarne in about 830, were brought the remains of St Ceolwulf, the pious king to whom the Venerable Bede dedicated his history, and the body of St Cuthbert rested here for a time during the course of its long, meandering journey. In 1083 the church was given into the protection of the Benedictine monastery established at Durham, and the existing church is thought to have been started by Bishop Flambard.

The church, though (like too many others) it has suffered from the hands of the restorer, is still impressive. It was planned from the beginning with full-length aisles to the nave and chancel, and the chancel, built by Bishop de Puiset in 1165, originally ended in an apse, but this was dismantled in favour of the present square end early in the fourteenth century. The south aisle was rebuilt in 1845 and the north aisle restored, with a new arcade, six years later, so the only parts surviving of the Norman building are the chancel, with the chancel arch (but excluding, of course, the east end), and the south arcade, but these are easily the finest parts of the church. The elaborately-carved seventeenth-century pulpit and stall were brought from Durham Cathedral. The church was more than once occupied as a base from which to besiege the castle, and it was here in 1291 that Edward I opened the momentous convention to weigh the rival claims of Baliol and Bruce to the throne of Scotland.

Norham Bridge, a sturdy structure built in 1887, crosses the Tweed into Scotland. High up on the bank on that side is the church of Ladykirk, supposed to owe its foundation in 1500 to James IV, who, when in danger from drowning while attempting to ford the river, vowed to build a church to the Virgin Mary should he come safely to land. The church was completed in about 1510 and James probably worshipped here on his way to Flodden Field. The architecture, showing marked French influences, is in distinct contrast to the restrained style of Norham church opposite. The most significant feature is the unbroken stone vault, a French custom that was adopted and developed in Scotland, though examples are to be seen at Bellingham and elsewhere in Northumberland. The tower was added in 1743 and is attributed to William Adam, the father of Robert.

About 3 miles above Norham Bridge, the Tweed is joined by the Till, its only important English tributary. In its lower reaches the Till is a deep, quiet river, flowing through a narrow, wooded ravine:

> *Tweed says to Till,*
> *'What gars ye rin sae still?'*
> *Says Till to Tweed,*
> *'Though ye rin wi' speed*

And aa rin slaw,
Whar ye droon yin man aa droon twa.'

It is difficult to realise that this dark and sluggish water began its course as a clear and sparkling burn in the Cheviot Hills.

The road from Berwick to Kelso crosses the Till at the fifteenth-century Twizel Bridge (pronounced 'Twy-'), with a bold span of 90 feet, of 'stone one bow, but greate and stronge', wrote the sixteenth-century traveller John Leland. It was across this bridge that James IV, either from an inferior knowledge of military tactics or (more probably) from a misplaced sense of chivalry, allowed the English vanguard to pass unmolested on the morning of the Battle of Flodden Field. Standing up on the right bank of the Till are the ruins of Twizel Castle, built only in the eighteenth century (despite its Norman-looking architecture), though it occupies the site of a castle 'caste downe' by James IV when he ravaged Northumberland in 1497.

Upstream on the banks of the Till are two villages that may claim to be among the most charming in the Border. That of Etal (pronounced 'E-tal') consists of a single street of whitewashed cottages, some old, some relatively new (one is dated 1935), and mostly of one storey. Some of the cottages have thatched roofs (uncommon in the Border) and some have roofs of large grey slabs, the whole surrounded by trees in the most delightful manner. The manor house, at the east end, is a graceful eighteenth-century Border residence. On a green bank above the river are the ruins of Etal Castle, built in 1342 in the quadrangular style met with at Chillingham, but laid waste by James IV during his incursion of 1497. The chief surviving features are the gatehouse-tower on the south-east and the Great Tower at the opposite corner. Heatherslaw Mill, an old corn--mill on the other side of the Till, farther up, has been restored as an agricultural museum.

Farther on is Ford, an estate village laid out after 1859 for Louisa, Marchioness of Waterford; its houses, mostly of a pleasing brown stone, have red-tiled roofs that tone well with their leafy surroundings. The former school is decorated with a series of frescoes of Biblical characters painted between 1861 and 1882 by the Marchioness, who employed many of the villagers and their children as her models. The Marchioness, who was a friend of the Pre-Raphaelite Brotherhood, lived just below the village, at Ford Castle, fortified in 1338 by Sir William Heron, High Sheriff of Northumberland, and perhaps the earliest example of the quadrangular style. The castle was partly rebuilt in the eighteenth century and again in 1861–65, but it still incorporates three of its fourteenth-century corner towers. The Early English church of Ford, farther down, was much altered in 1853, but retains a sturdy thirteenth-century bell-cote, mounted on a massive buttress of its west gable, like that of Holy Island. It looks out across the valley of the Till to Flodden Hill, where the Scottish forces were encamped on the night of 8 September 1513, before the Battle of Flodden Field.

The battle was fought, as is now well known, not at Flodden, but on an entirely different site some distance away, on the slopes above the village of Branxton. In importance it is raised well above the numerous Border forays by being not a mere skirmish between rival families and their followers, but a pitched engagement involving the armies of two nations. Henry VIII, with the main body of the English army, was abroad on an expedition in France when James IV (persuaded, it is believed, by the invitation of the Queen of France) crossed the Tweed at Coldstream with a large army to create a diversion in favour of the French and at the same time settle some differences he himself had with the English. He ensconced his forces at first in a strong position on the top of Flodden Hill (at that time bare of trees), where he was faced with an army comprised mainly of Northerners, hurriedly gathered together by the Earl of Surrey, then Lord Warden of the Marches.

The earl, after his offer to engage immediately with the Scots on the wide levels of Milfield Plain had been refused, decided on an absurdly daring stratagem. He moved his army back across the Till, and the following morning divided it into two, the artillery recrossing the Till lower down, at Twizel Bridge, while the rearguard forded the river near Crookham, between Ford and Branxton. The object of this manoeuvre was to cut off the Scots from their home country, and James, either because a drizzling rain was falling at the time and he was misinformed of the English movements or from a quixotic streak in his nature which impelled him to meet the enemy on equal terms, made no attempt to interfere with their plan. Instead, he deserted his position on Flodden Hill for an inferior one on the ridge above Branxton, facing his native hills, to which many of the Scots were fated never to return.

The engagement began at about four in the afternoon, at long range to begin with, but James soon foolishly relinquished his advantageous position and rushed down the hill and the remainder of the fight was contested hand to hand. At first it swung to the advantage of the Scots, but when the Scottish centre was being forced back James committed his last act of folly; he descended from his horse and entered the fight like a common soldier. With this added to the other misfortunes of the Scots, the result of the engagement could no longer be in doubt. On the morning following the battle the field was strewn with the chivalry of Scotland; in addition to the king, his son the Archbishop of St Andrews and as many as 46 nobles and 9,000 men are said to have been slain. The spot where James is reputed to have fallen is marked by a simple granite cross of 1910, inscribed 'To the Brave of Both Nations'.

The road from Wooler, passing north of Branxton and the battlefield, joins the Berwick-Kelso road at the attractive village of Cornhill. The main Kelso road turns right to cross a broad and beautiful reach of the Tweed by the stout Coldstream Bridge, built by John Smeaton in 1763–66, but widened in 1961. At the small red-roofed toll-house, on the Scottish side of the river, the toll-keeper gave the same service to runaway couples until 1856 as the blacksmith at Gretna Green (Chapter 14). Lord Brougham, the Whig Lord Chancellor, who successfully opposed the divorce of George IV from Queen Caroline, was married here in 1819. The Nun's Walk, along the river bank, affords a grand view over the sweeping bend of the Tweed to the distant humps of the Cheviot Hills.

Coldstream, from its position overlooking the ancient ford, has always been a place of some importance, but most of the crossings of the Border at this point seem to have gone undisturbed, or at least unrecorded. The pleasant small town now has agricultural engineering works and a knitwear factory, but retains few signs of its long existence. Its fame is owed not to any Border affairs but to the regiment of Coldstream Guards, raised here in 1659 by General Monck, the supporter of Charles II. A plaque on the Guards' House, rebuilt in 1865, near the Market Place, indicates their original headquarters. The town is bounded on the west by the policies of The Hirsel, the seat of the Earls of Home (pronounced 'Hume'), whose wooded grounds enclose a small loch, now a sanctuary for water-fowl.

The road from Cornhill to Kelso keeps to the south side of the Tweed, skirting green haughs, the scene in 1018 of a skirmish in which the Scots, commanded by Malcolm II, defeated the English under the Saxon Earl of Northumberland. Beside the river, at the plain village of Wark-on-Tweed, are the extremely scanty remains of a royal stronghold that was among the most important in the Border. A motte-and-bailey castle, it was rebuilt by Henry II after 1157, when he regained possession of Northumberland. No fortress has so little to show of its past glory, though this is not surprising, as its prominent position 'exposed it to repeated hostilities, and its history from the twelfth century down to, at least, the sixteenth century, is perhaps without parallel for surprises, assaults, sieges, blockades, surrenders, evacuation, burnings, restorations, slaughter'.

The castle was stormed by the Scots no fewer than 11 times between 1136 and 1523, and seven of these attacks were successful. It was defended against David II in 1346 by the beautiful Countess of Salisbury, and Edward III, hastening to the castle's relief, was entertained at a ball by the countess. Retrieving that lady's garter, according to Froissart (but to no other historian), he uttered the words *Honi soit qui mal y pense* which subsequently became the motto of the Most Noble Order of the Garter. In 1523 the Earl of Surrey strengthened the defences against a siege by the Duke of Albany, the lord-governor of Scotland, and even in 1541 the castle could still be described as a 'jewell of noysance' against the Scots, but little remains today apart from the original motte and other earthworks.

Beyond the hamlet of Carham the road, crossing the small Redden Burn, unobtrusively enters Scotland. The complete absence of any marks of antiquity hereabouts is owed mainly to the fact that for a short space the Border is exceptionally vulnerable. For it is here that the boundary leaves the Tweed on its way southward to the Cheviot Hills. Our road goes through Sprouston, formerly a centre of weaving, and climbs to the village of Maxwellheugh, then turns down to the handsome bridge of 1803, designed by John Rennie, that crosses the river to Kelso.

CHAPTER ELEVEN

Kelso and Teviotdale

Kelso, described by Sir Walter Scott (perhaps not without bias) as 'the
most beautiful ... village in Scotland', is a delightful market town and
agricultural centre, with cobbled streets and many old houses. It is
enchantingly situated in a fine curve of the Tweed, just opposite the point
where the river is joined by its principal tributary, the Teviot (pronounced
'Tee-veot'). Kelso has one of the four great abbeys on the Scottish side of
the Border, the others being at Jedburgh, Dryburgh and Melrose.

Known in the twelfth century as Calkou, Kelso became a favourite
royal residence and the infant James III was crowned in the abbey in
1460. It was an important gathering place for Scottish armies on their
projected invasions of England, and more than one of the fruitless treaties
between the nations was signed here. From its close proximity to the
Border, Kelso suffered more than most places at the hands of English invaders. It was attacked and burned in 1522 and again by the ruthless
Earl of Hertford, when he laid waste the Scottish side of the Border in
1544–45. The 'Old Pretender' was proclaimed king as James VIII in the
market place in 1715, and in 1746 his son, Prince Charles Edward
Stuart, stayed for two nights here on his retreat from over the Border.

The Square, the exceptionally wide cobbled market place, so different
from the usual narrow streets of a Border town, has suggested to more
than one writer the atmosphere of a French town rather than a Scottish
one, and a Continental-looking hotel adds to that impression. The curfew
is still rung each evening from the classical eighteenth-century Court
House. In Roxburgh Street, to the north-west, a horseshoe in the road,
outside a brewer's storehouse, marks the spot where Prince Charles's

147

horse cast a shoe while he was leaving Kelso. Chalkheugh Terrace, on the west farther on, affords a charming view of the rich pastures and woodlands bordering the Tweed and the Teviot. Walton Hall, at the head of Roxburgh Street (which leads to the gates of Floors Castle), is a small Regency house built for John Ballantyne, the friend and colleague of Scott.

The octagonal Parish Church of 1773, south-east of The Square, contains the family pews of the Duke of Roxburghe (who lives at Floors Castle) and the Douglases of Springwood Park. In The Knowes, farther south-east, a bust of Scott marks the house (formerly called Garden Cottage) where he lodged with 'his kind and affectionate aunt Janet' while attending the grammar school. Ednam House, a fine mansion of 1761 (now a hotel), with charming grounds descending to the Tweed, was previously the dower-house of the Dukes of Roxburghe.

Near the bridge are the splendid ruins of Kelso Abbey, one of the earliest of the many founded by David I, that 'sair sanct for the crown' (as James VI called him). It was settled in 1128 by monks of a reformed Benedictine order from Tiron, in Picardy, who had been at Selkirk since 1113. Henry, Earl of Northumberland, the founder's son, was buried here in 1152, and the abbey, profiting by the royal favour, soon rose to a position of wealth and influence. Its abbots, who were bishops also from 1165, juggled for supreme precedence with the bishops of St Andrews, the recognised ecclesiastical capital of Scotland, until James I in 1420 gave a decision against them. The abbey was garrisoned as a fortress when the Earl of Hertford came in 1545, and the towers were converted into strong-points, but on its capture by the English forces both the garrison and the monks were put to the sword and the monastery was reduced to its present state. At the Dissolution the abbey and its lands were conferred on Sir Robert Ker of Cessford, the ancestor of the Dukes of Roxburghe.

Architecturally, the ruins show a combination of the Norman (or Romanesque) style and the early Gothic (called the First Pointed style in Scotland). It was long thought that the remains were those of a relatively unimportant church, but the discovery of a description made in 1517 has proved that this was most likely the finest and largest of all the Border abbeys. The church was in the form of a double cross, about 300 feet long, with transepts at both ends (an arrangement unique in Scotland) and towers above the crossings rising to some 100 feet above the ground. Of this, however, only the west end has survived. The magnificent façade has part of a square Galilee porch with remains of a deeply moulded doorway of six arches or orders. Above the crossing are two sides of the west tower, supported by huge arches, 45 feet high. The two surviving bays of the south arcade have circular piers and above these are a triforium and clerestory of small arches. The splendid Norman façade of the north-west transept has a fine doorway with an ornamental arcade and a diapered gable above, and an unusual gable-like structure at the top between two turrets. This transept was used as the parish church of Kelso from 1645 until 1771. Around the walls of the church, at ground-floor level, ran an elegant interlaced arcade.

On the site of the nave stood the grammar school attended by Walter Scott for six months in 1783. Fellow pupils were the brothers James and John Ballantyne, natives of the town, and the friendship that developed fixed the first bond of a partnership that was to have such momentous results. It was from Kelso in 1802 that the newly-formed Ballantyne Press issued the first two volumes of Scott's *Minstrelsy of the Scottish Border*. On the school wall east of the abbey church is a memorial to Captain Robert Scott, who died in 1804, Sir Walter's uncle, whom he often visited at Rosebank, three-quarters of a mile out of the town on the Coldstream road. An early-Gothic arch on the south of the church forms the entrance to a Romanesque-style cloister, built by the Duchess of Roxburghe in 1929 as a family memorial and burial place.

From the bridge we have a fine view of the abbey ruins and also of Floors Castle, upstream; the imposing entrance gates of 1929 are on the Lauder road, half a mile from the town centre. The palatial mansion of the Ker family (pronounced 'Kar'), Dukes of Roxburghe since 1707, was built in 1718 by Sir John Vanbrugh and altered by W. H. Playfair in about 1849 to its present neo-Tudor style, with numerous turrets. It is 'so situated as to combine the ideas of ancient baronial grandeur with those of modern taste'. In the large park, which is bordered by the Tweed, is a holly-tree said to mark the place where James II, while besieging Roxburgh Castle in 1460, was killed by the bursting of a 'misframit gun', which he was inspecting 'mair curieous nor becam him or the majestie of ane King'.

The road for Melrose and Selkirk, turning right from the south end of

Kelso Bridge, skirts the beautiful grounds of Springwood Park and crosses the Teviot. In a green haugh whose banks are watered by both the Teviot and the Tweed are still held, on the second Friday in September, the Kelso Ram Sales, maintaining the tradition of the great St James's Fair which first took place in the reign of David I. The tolls of the fair were collected, oddly enough, by the provost and bailies of Jedburgh, about 11 miles away, a state of affairs that often caused much ill-feeling between the two towns.

On a narrow grassy ridge between the two rivers are the remains of Roxburgh Castle, consisting of a few walls of the bailey. The ruin stands on a high bank that drops steeply to the Teviot and is protected on its other sides by a wide ditch previously flooded with water from the river. In the castle, once an important royal residence, Alexander II was married in 1221 and Alexander III was born in 1241. No place, with the exception of Berwick, suffered so much and so often from the internecine strife of the Border during the Middle Ages; it was continually under siege and was as frequently changing hands. The castle had been in the possession of the English for the best part of a hundred years when the queen of James II, capturing it after his death, decided that nothing less than its complete destruction would effectively remove this perpetual menace to the Scots.

No trace at all survives of the once-important town of Roxburgh, which stood on the neck of the narrow isthmus between the Teviot and the Tweed. One of the four royal burghs that established a convention or court in the thirteenth century, it rivalled Edinburgh, Stirling and Berwick in importance. But neither Carthage nor Babylon has disappeared more completely; not a stone, not a mound, now remains to mark the site. Its streets, its churches, its convent, its mint (where many Scottish coins were struck), all have vanished as effectively as if they had never existed.

A road turns up the west side of the Teviot to the small village of Roxburgh, charmingly situated near the river, with a church built in 1752 but since restored. In the churchyard is buried Andrew Gemmels, who died in 1793 at the age of 106. The original of Edie Ochiltree, the bedesman in Scott's novel *The Antiquary*, he lived at the farm of Roxburgh Newtown, near the Selkirk road.

Another road from Kelso, via Maxwellheugh, runs up the east and south sides of the Teviot, which rises on the bare hills above Eskdale and takes an almost direct course north-eastward for over 30 miles before joining the Tweed. It flows through one of the most characteristic of the Border valleys, pastoral rather than rugged in nature, and is itself fed by some considerable streams, of which the most notable are the Kale Water and the Jed Water, descending from the Border hills, the Ale Water, winding across the uplands on the other bank, and the Borthwick Water, above Hawick.

The first of the Teviot's tributaries to be crossed is the Kale Water, and a road turns up its open valley towards Town Yetholm, with the triple-peaked Eildon Hills in full view behind. Beyond the road junction is the restored eighteenth-century church of Eckford (the village is more than half a mile farther on), with a contemporary laird's loft or gallery, a peculiarly Scottish feature. On the outside wall hang the iron 'jougs' or bridle, of 1718, in which were pilloried offenders found guilty of breaking the Sabbath by the dreaded Kirk Sessions who presided over religious life in the eighteenth century. In the churchyard is a round watch-tower, built not as a lookout for raiders from over the Border, but to guard against the depredations of body-snatchers.

A road on the right of the Kale Water road leads to the hamlet of Cessford, on a tributary stream. To the north are the massive ruins of the castle, a stronghold of the Kers (ancestors of the Duke of Roxburghe), who were as notorious as freebooters in this part of the Border as were the Armstrongs in Liddesdale. The castle, which has walls 14 feet thick, was surrendered to the English under the Earl of Hertford in 1545.

The valley road continues to Morebattle (the 'botl', or abode, by the mere), at the edge of the Cheviot Hills, where the Kale Water makes a sharp turn from north to west. Linton, a mile north, beyond the river, has a church practically rebuilt in 1912, but retaining its twelfth-century font and a tympanum or carved panel above the door said to portray Sir John Somerville, who was knighted by William the Lion (1165–1214), slaying a 'ravening beast'.

From the road eastward, which crosses the watershed to the Bowmont Valley (Chapter 6), a quiet road ascends the Kale Water, skirting the Cheviot Hills on their western side. In its upper course this is a typical moorland burn, but the valley it threads differs from others in the

Cheviots in being frequently enriched by a profusion of foliage, while the flanking hills are rather less high and less steep. On Hownam Law (1472 feet), between the Kale Water and the Bowmont Water, is a large Iron Age hill-fort with a massive wall about 10 feet thick, enclosing traces of the shallow platforms of saucer-like depressions of numerous houses.

The road leads to the remote village of Hownam (pronounced 'Hou-'), a haunt in the seventeenth century of the persecuted Covenanters, Presbyterian adherents to the National Covenant who were seeking to worship in liberty. Built into the walls of the small church, by the tree-embowered river, are some old tombstones, an economy not infrequently met with on this side of the Border. The old drove road known as 'The Street', crossing the Border to Coquetdale (Chapter 5), starts here and passes to the south of the hill-fort of Hownam Rings, the excavation of which, in 1948, revealed a whole series of settlements and paved the way to an understanding of prehistoric building methods over more than 500 years.

To the south of Hownam the valley of the Kale Water changes character, becoming of a more open, moorland nature. On a low ridge to the west, near the derelict farm of Pennymuir, at the junction of roads to Oxnam, are the rectangular earthworks of a sequence of large Roman marching camps. They stood beside Dere Street, which came down over the north side of Woden Law from Blackhall Hill on the Border (Chapter 5) and can be explored northward as a farm track to its junction with a road from Hownam to Jedburgh. On Woden Law (1388 feet), a distinctive flat-topped hill to the east of the valley, are the ramparts and ditches of an Iron Age hill-fort, partly enclosed by the banks and ditches of Roman siege works, perhaps made as training exercises by the army billeted at Pennymuir. From its position on the edge of the Cheviots, the law affords a wide view over Teviotdale to the Eildons and the Lammermuirs. The valley road goes on to the last farms of Nether and Upper Hindhope, from which tracks climb to the Border near the head of the Coquet west of the Chew Green forts (Chapter 5).

The road from Pennymuir turns northward down the open upper valley of the Oxnam Water (pronounced 'Ooze-nam' locally), which runs roughly parallel to the Kale Water. The secluded village of Oxnam, among low green hills, has a church of 1738 with the iron jougs still hanging on the outside wall, as at Eckford. To the north of Oxnam the road divides, the left branch crossing a ridge to Jedburgh (Chapter 13), while the right branch goes on north past the farm of Cappuck, just beyond which is the site of a small Roman fort. It has been excavated and sculptures have been found, but practically nothing is now to be seen above ground. The fort stood just south of Dere Street, the course of which can be followed as farm roads in both directions. From Crailinghall our road leaves the valley and continues north to reach the Kelso-Hawick road south of Eckford.

The road up the south side of Teviotdale goes through the scattered village of Crailing, on the Oxnam Water above its junction with the Teviot. Nisbet, on the north side of the river, was the birthplace in about 1600 of Samuel Rutherford, the theologian. Educated at Edinburgh University, he was appointed regent or professor of humanity there in 1623. He was dismissed from his post because of an alleged indiscretion before his marriage, but in 1627 he became minister of Anwoth in Kirkcudbrightshire. In 1636 Rutherford was deposed, because of his non-conformist views, and sentenced to confinement in Aberdeen during the king's pleasure. In 1638, on the re-establishment of Presbyterianism, he was appointed professor of divinity at St Andrews and in 1643 he was one of the Scottish commissioners at the signing in London of the Solemn League and Covenant (whereby the Scottish covenanters promised military aid to the English parliament in return for the establishment of Presbyterianism in England). Rutherford became principal of St Mary's College, St Andrews, and later of New College there. At the Restoration of Charles II in 1660 he was deprived of all his offices, his works were burned by the common hangman and he was cited to appear before parliament on a charge of high treason, but his death in 1661 prevented this from taking effect.

Above the Teviot farther on rises the rocky hill of Peniel Heugh (777 feet), commanding charming views both up and down Teviotdale. On the top are two hill-forts and a prominent monument raised in 1815 by the Marquess of Lothian and his tenants in celebration of the Duke of Wellington's famous victory at Waterloo. At the southern foot of the hill are the finely-wooded grounds of Monteviot House, the Scottish seat of the Kerr family (pronounced 'Kar'), Marquesses of Lothian since 1701.

The main road crosses the Jed Water to Bonjedward, where the road to Jedburgh bears to the left. We continue on the south of the Teviot for a mile, then turn right from the Hawick road to cross the river and skirt the Ale Water; its name, like those of Aln and Alwin over the Border, signifies white, and it is a quiet river, flowing 'the green hills under'. Ancrum, an attractive village on a knoll above a crook of the Ale Water, has brown-stone houses and a thirteenth-century market cross. To the north of the village the river is lined by steep red-sandstone cliffs, with several caves, in one of which James Thomson, the poet (who was born in the manse at Ednam, near Kelso), is said to have carved his name. To the north of the river stretches the windswept Ancrum Moor, traversed by the road to Melrose and by Dere Street on its way to Newstead, on the Tweed. In 1545 the English invaders were returning over the moor from a raid, laden with booty, when they were waylaid by the Scots and heavily defeated, their leaders, Sir Ralph Evers and Sir Bryan Latoun, being among the slaughtered.

The Hawick road, continuing up the south side of Teviotdale, next crosses the Rule Water, which flows through a quiet and little-known glen from Bonchester Bridge (Chapter 13). The small village of Bedrule, on the east of the wooded glen, was the birthplace of William Turnbull, appointed Bishop of Glasgow in 1447 and the founder of Glasgow University, in 1450. Above the glen to the west rise the 'stormy skirts' of Rubers Law (1392 feet), a distinctive conical hill that has a reputation for encouraging bad weather. The rugged granite summit of this height, the 'dark Ruberslaw' of *Marmion*, was a favourite retreat of the persecuted Covenanters, to whom Alexander Peden preached from a crag known as 'Peden's Pulpit', being saved from the pursuing dragoons on one occasion by a characteristic mist which descended suddenly over the summit. The fort crowning the hill consists of two enclosures, one within the other and of different periods; the inner wall, probably later than about A.D. 200, is remarkable in incorporating re-used Roman stones.

The Teviotdale road goes through Denholm, a village built round a large square green on which is a monument of 1861 to John Leyden, the poet and orientalist, who was born in a thatched cottage to the north-east in 1775, the son of a shepherd. A brilliant scholar, he became a licentiate of the church in 1800, but continued his linguistic and scientific studies. He was a fast friend of Scott and contributed to the *Minstrelsy of the Scottish Border*. Leyden visited India, Malaya and the East Indian islands, collecting linguistic and ethnographical knowledge, and he was appointed professor in the Bengal College and a judge in Calcutta. In 1811 he accompanied the governor-general of India to Java, but died there after three days of a fever, at the age of 36.

To the north of Denholm, beyond the Teviot, rise the twin humps of the Minto Hills (905 feet). The hamlet of Hassendean, below their south-west foot, is immortalised in the stirring ballad of *Jock o' Hazeldean*. Minto House, below the hills on the east, was built in 1814 and is now Craigmount School. It replaces a house that belonged to the Turnbulls and later came to the Elliots, the best known of whom is Jean or Jane, born here in 1725, who wrote that undying version of the lament for Flodden, *The Flowers of the Forest*. Farther east, on the steep wooded Minto Crags, is the medieval pele tower of Fatlips Castle, the stronghold of the Turnbulls, a lawless clan that demanded tribute from all this part of the Border until crushed by James IV.

On a ridge south of the Teviotdale road (but out of sight from it) are the ruins of Cavers House, once the principal seat of the 'black' Douglases, built about 1400 by the son of that Douglas who fell at Otterburn. The Douglases, with the Scotts and the Kers, were the most powerful families on the Scottish side of the Border. From them were usually chosen the Wardens of the Marches, but they could be little trusted to dispense justice in that office, as they themselves were often raiding the English when not squabbling with each other, and they were far more disposed to rely on the axe and the sword to maintain order than to trust to settlement by arbitration, as their position demanded. But while the Scotts and the Kers climbed slowly to power and dignity, their chiefs finally attaining to rank and title, the Douglases, the most influential family in Scotland in the early fifteenth century, overstepped their bounds and pushed their claims as rivals to the Stewarts for the crown of Scotland, until effectively subjected by James II. In 1455 the Earl of Douglas received a grant of a pension of £500 a year from the English king, 'to be paid for services to be rendered by him, until he should recover the whole, or the greatest part of his possessions, which had been taken from him by the person *who called himself king of Scotland*'. But the ambitious Douglas soon met with two great reverses, first in Eskdale, then in the Berwickshire Merse, after which the power of the family declined. The house is fast decaying, and even the old church of 1662, which incorporates a burial aisle of the Elliots, is no longer used.

The road from Kelso, joined by a road from Carter Bar and Bonchester Bridge, goes on south of the Teviot to enter the main street of Hawick (Chapter 14).

CHAPTER TWELVE

The Scott Country

Above Kelso, between St Boswells and the junction of the Ettrick Water, the Tweed makes a noble sweep round the base of the triple-peaked Eildon Hills, past Sir Walter Scott's home at Abbotsford and the beautiful abbey of Melrose, under the grand view-point of Bemersyde Hill, and past the secluded ruins of Dryburgh Abbey, the burial-place of Scott. There is no doubt in my mind that this part of the Tweed valley, embracing the region popularly known as the Scott Country, would have achieved a high reputation for its natural charm, even if it had not been touched by the magic wand of the great romancer. But though the many visitors who flock in summer to this comparatively small area of the Border (when by far the greater part of it remains neglected) may be enticed to some extent by the undoubted beauty of the Tweed and the splendid ruins of Melrose and Dryburgh, far more are inveigled here by the romantic spell that the 'Wizard of the North' has woven round it.

Scotland's good fortune in having fathered a man of the character and ability of Sir Walter Scott is one of the main reasons why the Scottish side of the Border is much better known than the English. In the first chapter, I said it was a tragedy that Northumberland had nurtured no major poet who could, using the dialect, express the feelings and share the experience of his people (Swinburne, though of Northumbrian extraction, wasted his great talents in this direction). But even if such a poet had developed, it is unlikely that he would have achieved the immense and lasting reputation of Scott. For one thing, the English are markedly less patriotic than the Scots; if Sir Walter had been the product of the southern side of the Border, his memorial would not be seen everywhere in Northumbrian towns or his bust in numerous hotels and private houses. And for another, the Englishman rarely feels excited or saddened by the events of his country's past history, while the Scotsman hardly for a moment forgets his. As Andrew and John Lang pointed out in *Highways and Byways in the Border*, 'when Bannockburn and Ancrum Moor are mentioned Englishmen "kept more than usual calm", whereas to the Scot, Flodden and Pinkie are perpetual sorrows'.

The road from Kelso on the north side of the Tweed follows for several miles the stout wall that bounds the large park of Floors Castle (Chapter 11). Then, bearing left from the Earlston road, it passes south of the hill on which stands the stark ruin of Smailholm Tower, rising aloof from a rugged pinnacle of rock and mirrored in the clear waters of a small loch. This fifteenth-century pele-tower, 57 feet high and commanding a wide view across the Tweed to the Cheviots, played a not inconsiderable part in the early development of Scott, for up to the age of eight he spent much time with his paternal grandfather at the near-by farmhouse of Sandyknowe. Here he first absorbed the Border legends and ballads and the tales of ancient forays, and Smailholm enters into the early ballad of *The Eve of St John*, as well as into the third canto of *Marmion*.

The road descends to the Tweed at Mertoun Bridge, passing the entrance to Mertoun House, on a broad reach of the river, a classical house begun in 1703 for Sir William Scott of Harden (near Hawick), the branch of the family that included Sir Walter, and their seat after they had 'warstled up the brae' to an earldom. The church near by, rebuilt in 1658, but restored in 1820 and again in 1898, retains its seventeenth-century belfry, and in the finely-wooded park are the former, seventeenth-century, house and a doocot (dovecot) of 1576. The ruined Littledean Tower, on the other bank of the Tweed downstream, was once a stronghold of the warlike Kers.

St Boswells, to the west of Mertoun Bridge, takes its name from Boisil, the prior of Old Melrose to whom the youthful Cuthbert came, exchanging the crook for the cowl. Its previous name was Lessudden, supposed to be derived in turn from St Aidan, Cuthbert's forerunner as Bishop of Lindisfarne and traditionally the founder of the monastery of Old Melrose. The large village, built mostly of the local red sandstone, consists mainly of one long street, leading to a wide common (St Boswell's Green), famous for its sheep fair, held annually in July. Newtown St Boswells, a mile farther on towards Melrose, began as a railway village centred on an important junction; it became the county town of Roxburghshire when the new offices were built here, and is now the administrative centre of the new region known as The Borders.

Upstream from Mertoun Bridge, and reached by a quiet road on the east side of the Tweed, are the ruins of Dryburgh Abbey, on a verdant strath enclosed in a loop of the wide, rushing river. Dryburgh is the most beautifully situated if not the most extensive of the Border abbeys, but it is perhaps visited not so much for its lovely setting or for the graceful architecture of its remains, but to pay homage at the shrine of Sir Walter Scott, who was buried here in 1832, within sound of the Tweed, that dearest of all sounds to his ear.

The abbey was founded in 1150, probably by Hugo de Moreville, the lord of Lauderdale and constable of Scotland, for Premonstratensian canons from Alnwick Abbey across the Border. It suffered frequently at the hands of the invading English; it was thrown down by Edward II in 1322 and by Richard II in 1385, and after a further devastation in 1544 by the hated Earl of Hertford, it was never rebuilt. The remains belong chiefly to the Transitional period of architecture, blending the rounded Norman or Romanesque arch with the pointed Early English (called the First Pointed style in Scotland). Of the church, secluded among yews and other conifers, there survives part of the west front, rebuilt after 1385 with a fine round-headed doorway, fragments of the nave and aisles (mostly of the fifteenth century) and parts of the late twelfth-century choir and presbytery and the south transept, from which a night-stair ascends to the ruined dormitory of the canons.

But the best preserved portions of the church are the east aisle of the north transept and the adjoining chapel of the presbytery. In the chapel is the tomb of Sir Walter Scott, and here also are buried his wife, Charlotte Charpentier (called Carpenter on her monument), who died in 1826, his elder son, and his biographer and son-in-law, John Gibson Lockhart, who died in 1854. In the north transept is the grave of Field-Marshal Earl Haig, commander of the British forces in the First World War. Only the Scotts of Abbotsford, the Haigs of Bemersyde, and the Erskines, Earls of Buchan, have the right of sepulture in the abbey.

The cloister, with the exceptionally complete conventual buildings, largely of the late twelfth century, is placed at a lower level than the church and is reached from the nave by steps through a noble round-headed doorway. On the east side are the Library and Vestry (altered after 1786 as the burial-place of the Erskines) and the barrel-vaulted Chapter House, still complete, with another fine doorway and part of its arcading, and some traces of early wall painting, a rarity in Scottish ecclesiastical buildings. Farther south are the Calefactory, or warming-house, and the Novices' Day Room; and in the south range is the Refectory, in the west gable of which is a beautiful fifteenth-century rose window. To the south-west of the cloisters are remains of a small late fifteenth-century gatehouse, formerly the entrance to the abbey.

The three-mile stretch of the Tweed between Dryburgh and the confluence of the Leader is perhaps the most exquisite reach of the river, running between red sandstone outcrops or bounded by steep curving banks quite overhung by rich woods. The road from the abbey climbs up to Bemersyde (the first 'e' is pronounced long), a hamlet adjoining the grounds of Bemersyde House, the hereditary home of the Haig family, who have held the property for over 800 years, thus bearing out a prophecy made by Thomas of Earlston (Thomas the Rhymer), who declared that 'Tyde what may betyde, Haig shall be Haig of Bemersyde'. The Haigs were always a force to contend with in the Border; there was scarcely a skirmish in which the family did not take part, often to leave at least one member on the field, and Field-Marshal Douglas Haig was the successor of this powerful line. The house, mainly of the eighteenth century, but incorporating a sixteenth-century tower, was bought by national subscription and gifted in 1921 to Earl Haig, who died here in 1928.

The road going on north for Leaderfoot crosses the flank of Bemersyde Hill (1747 feet), which commands a splendid panorama famous as the favourite view of Sir Walter Scott. The story told by Lockhart can never be too often repeated; of how, when Scott was being taken this way on his last journey from Abbotsford to Dryburgh, the horses which were drawing the hearse paused at this spot, as they had been in the habit of doing for many years, to allow Sir Walter to admire the view. A house on the green haugh below, almost encircled by a magnificent loop of the Tweed, marks the site of Old Melrose (or Mailros), a Celtic or Culdee monastery founded, it is believed, by St Aidan, in the 7th century. St Cuthbert, born in the Lammermuirs in about 625, became a monk here in 651.

The charming prospect from Scott's View is dominated by the triple summits of the Eildons, beyond the Tweed, but includes also the dark Rubers Law and the rounded Minto Hills, to the south, with the hills above Teviotdale and Liddesdale farther off; Ettrick Forest, to the south-west; and the hills around the upper Tweed to the west. I have viewed a great many celebrated views, both in these islands and abroad, but that from Bemersyde Hill is, in my opinion, not easily excelled. Perhaps the prospect is most exciting on a clear day in winter, when more of the Tweed is visible (the leaves being off the trees) and snow drapes the distant hills of Ettrick Forest, silhouetting them in white and making the Eildons stand out like the prongs of Neptune's trident.

From Bemersyde Hill a road descends to cross the Leader Water just above the point where it flows into the Tweed. The main Edinburgh-Jedburgh-Newcastle road crosses the major river by a new bridge, close by the narrow but graceful old bridge, upstream of which are the tall arches of an imposing railway viaduct. The road on the south side of the Tweed passes a monument marking the site of the Roman fort of *Trimontium*, taking its name naturally from the Eildons which dominated it. The fort stood on Dere Street, the road from *Corstopitum* to Cramond, on the Firth of Forth (see Chapter 4). Built in about A.D. 80 by Agricola, after he had forced his way through this difficult and inhospitable country, the fort was deserted between about 100 and 140, but was rebuilt and was in use again until about 180, when it was finally abandoned and the Romans retreated to the more easily defensible line of Hadrian's Wall. The remains have been thoroughly excavated (the finds are in the National Museum of Antiquities in Edinburgh) and as efficiently covered over again, so that nothing is now to be seen above the surface. But a fine view opens up the Tweed from the site, past Melrose Abbey to the distant mill chimneys of Galashiels.

Beyond the village of Newstead the valley broadens out into a rich strath, overlooked by the venerable ruins of Melrose Abbey, well placed above the south bank of the Tweed, but hustled by the houses of the town that has grown up alongside the abbey. Melrose, however, has escaped the smudge of industrialism that has descended on Hawick and Galashiels and even, to a lesser extent, on Selkirk and Jedburgh; the little grey town, grouped round its triangular market place, still conveys the atmosphere of older and simpler days, and to enter Melrose is to sample in some measure the flavour of medieval times. In the Market Square is a seventeenth-century mercat cross bearing the weathered arms of Scotland. The 'Kennaquhair' of Scott's *The Monastery* and *The Abbot* (both set in the sixteenth century), Melrose is the best centre for the exploration of the country intimately associated with the great novelist.

Melrose Abbey, eloquently described in *The Lay of the Last Minstrel*, is not as exquisitely situated as Dryburgh or even as outwardly impressive as Jedburgh, but it makes up for these defects by the beauty and delicacy of its architectural detail, which place it in the front rank of Scottish monastic buildings. Founded and endowed in 1136 by David I, in succession to the Celtic monastery of Old Melrose, it was the first Cistercian monastery established in Scotland. Settled with monks brought from Rievaulx in Yorkshire, Melrose was dedicated in 1146. Alexander II was buried here in 1249, but the abbey unhappily lay in the direct path of English invasion; it was devastated again and again, especially by Edward II in 1322 and Richard II in 1385. Robert Bruce made a grant to restore it in 1326 and (says tradition) bequeathed his heart to it, but the abbey was mostly rebuilt after 1385, under the direction of Jean Moreau, one of the French master-masons who greatly influenced Scottish architecture. Partly rebuilt again in the mid-fifteenth century, the abbey was finally plundered and wasted in the Earl of Hertford's invasions of 1544–45.

The beautiful ruins (best viewed, according to Scott, by moonlight) date largely from the fifteenth century. They comprise the east part of the nave of the church, with a row of burial chapels opening from the south aisle, the transepts, part of the central tower, and the chancel or presbytery. Almost every detail of these is worth the most careful consideration. The capitals of the piers, for example, reveal the masterly skill of the Scottish stone-carvers of the time, especially in the delicate foliage showing the leaves of the 'curly kale'. Of the chapels built on to the south aisle in the early sixteenth century, eight remain, with windows displaying rich and varied Decorated or Second Pointed tracery. The north aisle, which is unusually narrow, abuts against the cloister. An early fifteenth-century stone pulpitum or screen separates the west end of the nave (or lay-brothers' choir) from the monks' choir, which extends for three bays into the nave and which has graceful arches obscured on the north side by the massive arcade built in 1618, when the choir was altered to serve as a Presbyterian church. Two piers of the tower, with clustered shafts, survive at the crossing. The transepts have east aisles and clerestory windows with inner arcades, and off the north transept opens the sacristy. The south transept has a splendid Decorated window with flowing tracery, and on the south front outside are niches, some with beheaded figures. The north transept has an unusual 'crown of thorns' window.

The presbytery has an elaborate stone-vaulted ceiling, with bosses, and windows of after 1385 with tracery perhaps inserted by Jean Moreau, master-mason at Melrose in the early fifteenth century, referred to as 'Morow' on a weathered tablet in the south transept. The magnificent Perpendicular east window, with its 'slender shafts of shapely stone', is of a design unusual for Scotland. The tombs of the Douglases below were wantonly defaced by Sir Ralph Evers during the Earl of Hertford's incursion of 1544, before he met just retribution on Ancrum Moor. The heart of Bruce, carried to Spain by Sir James Douglas, who died while on a pilgrimage to the Holy Land, is said to have been buried near the high altar, but excavation has revealed no trace of it. A tomb to the south of the chancel is supposed to be that of Michael Scot, whose scientific attainments and erudition in the early thirteenth century earned him the title of 'the Wizard'. It was his book of spells, buried with him, that occasioned the midnight visit of William of Deloraine to the abbey, described in *The Lay of the Last Minstrel*.

The cloisters have fine early thirteenth-century arcading, and at the east end of the south walk is a rich Decorated doorway with a round head. The ground plan of the claustral buildings has been laid bare by excavation, and beyond the lane north of the precinct are other foundations of domestic buildings, with the great drain for flushing the latrines. The Commendator's House here, built in 1590, has been restored as the abbey museum and contains finds made during the excavations, among them fragments of the shrine of St Waltheof, the second abbot, who died in 1159. He was the son of Queen Matilda of England, who afterwards married Prince David, later David I of Scotland. A commendator was in theory a monk who held a benefice *in commendam*, on the recommendation of the monarch. In practice the office was often awarded to laymen for services rendered; the Earl of Bothwell was made commendator of Melrose in 1566 by Queen Mary.

In the churchyard south of the nave is the tomb of Sir David Brewster, the physicist, famous for his discoveries concerning the diffraction and polarisation of light. He was born in Jedburgh in 1781, the son of the grammar-school master, and died in 1868 at his home at Allerly, near the village of Gattonside, north of the Tweed. To the south-east of the south transept is the grave of Tom Purdie, the wood-forester at Abbotsford and Scott's favourite henchman, and in the extreme south-west corner of the churchyard is the grave of his coachman, Peter Mathieson, who died in 1852 at the age of 84. An unusual procession, dating back to 1746, takes place on the evening of St John's Day (27th December), when members of the Masonic Lodge of Melrose proceed by torchlight from the mercat cross to the abbey and back again.

Melrose lies on the lowest slopes of the Eildon Hills (pronounced 'Eel-'), that trio of distinctive conical peaks which dominates the scene in this part of the Border (though the southernmost is hidden from Melrose itself). The Eildons are remarkable not only for their distinctive form and their isolated position, well away from any other group, but also for their being predominantly heather-covered in a landscape whose hills are main-ly of grass. The ascent of the central and highest peak (1385 feet) can be made comfortably in less than an hour. The view, as might be expected, is as extensive as any in the Border; Scott claimed that he could 'point out forty-three places famous in war and verse'. Around the north-east top (1327 feet) are the ramparts of a large hill-fort (of about 40 acres), the oppidum or headquarters of the Selgovae, occupied until the arrival of the Romans in A.D. 79.

From the south summit the descent may be made (though the track is not everywhere easy to find) to Bowden (pronounced 'Bow-' as in 'now'), a pleasant village with a green, lying at the foot of the hills. The name is derived from St Bothan, another monk of Old Melrose. The church, delightfully situated on a bank above a wood-shaded burn, was founded in 1128 by the monks of Kelso, but was mainly rebuilt in 1644 and much restored in 1909. Under the Cavers loft (or galleried pew) of 1661 is a curious inscription. In 1571 Bowden was granted a charter for a market, the first to be licensed in Scotland outside a burgh.

The road to the west from Melrose, passing near the parish church of 1810 (replacing the church in the abbey), runs north of the residential village of Darnick. Chiefswood, to the south beyond the railway, was built in 1810 by John Smith of Darnick for Scott's elder daughter, Sophia, and became the summer home of John Gibson Lockhart after their marriage in 1820, while Huntlyburn House, to the west, was the home of the staunch friend of Scott, Sir Adam Ferguson, who died in 1855. The Huntly Burn descends through the wooded Rhymer's Glen, where Thomas of Earlston or Ercildoune met the 'Queen of the Fairies'.

In the village is a tower of 1569 replacing an older tower (of 1425) that was destroyed by Hertford. The property of the Heiton family from the beginning, it is a good example of the typical Border pele (though restored), with battlements and crow-stepped gables. A Heiton of Darnick was among those who fell at Flodden Field, and another took part in that terrific encounter between the Scotts and the Elliots in 1526 on a near-by site since known as Skirmish Field, the stake being the custody of the young James V, as described by Scott in *The Monastery*. Sir Walter took a great interest in the tower when he was seeking a new residence as a successor to Ashiesteel farther up the Tweed, a fact that gained him the nickname of the 'Duke of Darnick'. But for better or worse he selected another site, a mile and a half upstream from Darnick, a farm known as Cartley Hole.

Scott bought the property, then 'small and poor', in 1811, changed its name to Abbotsford, and spent some £50,000 and the rest of his life in improving the estate and converting a simple dwelling into the magnificent baronial hall which he thought fitting to his position as a Border laird. From 1818 he began to enlarge the existing farmhouse, but in 1822 he demolished this in favour of a more elaborate mansion, begun by Edward Blore and completed in 1824 by William Atkinson. Ruskin described the house, not without justification, as 'perhaps the most incongruous pile that gentlemanly modernism ever designed'.

It is not, however, for its architecture that Abbotsford is visited as the most popular attraction in the Border, but for the lovable personality of its creator. The great rambling mansion, under its maze of turrets, gables and chimneys, is imbued with the atmosphere distilled by the inimitable romancer. Abbotsford still remains very largely as Scott left it at his death, except that a west wing was added after 1855 for J. R. Hope-Scott. In one or other of the houses here all the Waverley novels were written, from *Waverley* itself, published in 1814. When that appalling financial disaster overtook Scott in 1826, the house and library were generously spared him by his creditors, and on his death in 1832 they were ensured to his family by subscription. When Scott's last surviving son died childless in 1847, the property passed to his grandson, Walter Lockhart, younger brother of the 'Littlejohn' for whom the *Tales of a Grandfather* were written, and since then it has descended mostly in the female line, the additional name of Scott being added by each owner.

The grounds, sloping down to the murmuring Tweed, likewise show the hand of Scott. When he bought the estate it was 'as tame and uninteresting a stretch of ground as could well be met with', but he immediately set about planting it with trees, and the consequent change in the character of the landscape is due wholly to his foresight.

The house contains many personal memorials of Sir Walter, as well as gifts presented to him by famous people and a fascinating collection of Scottish historical relics made by him, revealing perfectly his character and interests. The Entrance Hall has panelling from the old kirk of Dunfermline (where Robert Bruce was buried), armorial bearings of Scottish Border families, and the last suit of clothes worn by Scott. Set into the wall outside, above and west of the porch, is the door of the old tolbooth or prison of Edinburgh, the 'Heart of Midlothian'. The Study, hardly altered since Scott's day, contains his writing-desk and armchair, and it needs but little imagination to visualise the master at work here, beginning his day at four o'clock in the morning. The Library holds some 9,000 of Scott's books, many of them with a markedly individual flavour, and has a carved ceiling modelled with designs from Roslin Chapel near Edinburgh. The bust of 1820 here, by Sir Francis Chantrey, is generally regarded as the best likeness of Scott. In the Drawing Room is a portrait of Sir Walter by Raeburn, and on the walls of the Armoury are Scottish weapons, including Rob Roy's gun, broadsword and dirk, and his sporran purse. The Dining Room contains portraits of Scott's wife and his younger daughter, Anne, as well as of his great-grandfather, Walter, nicknamed 'Beardie', who was 'out' in the Jacobite Rising of 1715 and who vowed never to shave until the Stuarts were restored to the throne. It was in this room, within sight and sound of his favourite river, that Sir Walter died, on a day in September 'so perfectly still', says Lockhart in his *Life*, 'that the sound of all others most delicious to his ear, the gentle ripple of the Tweed over its pebbles, was distinctly audible'.

CHAPTER THIRTEEN

From Jedburgh to Liddesdale

From Bonjedward (Chapter 11), on the Kelso-Hawick road through Teviotdale, the road to Jedburgh (and the Border) ascends the luxuriantly-wooded valley of the Jed Water, a delightful river whose head-streams are in Wauchope Forest, below the Border ridge. The road crosses the river twice in the narrow glen before reaching the High Street of the old town.

Jedburgh (pronounced '-bu-rur'), formerly the county town of Roxburghshire (the administrative offices are now at Newtown St Boswells, towards Melrose), is a market town and royal burgh famous for its noble abbey. Its old names included Jedward and Jedworth, the first element being derived probably from the Welsh 'gwd', meaning a twist or turn, an apt description for the winding Jed Water.

The chief place of the Middle Marches on the Scottish side, Jedburgh, from its proximity to the Border, was the scene of constant strife and bloodshed almost from its foundation in the 9th century. The town suffered severely at the hands of the English, notably in 1523, when it was attacked by the Earl of Surrey, and in 1544–45, when it was sacked and burned by the Earl of Hertford. But Jedburgh men acquired an unprecedented reputation for their courage; they were found engaged in many a Border skirmish, wielding to such purpose the 'Jeddart staff' (pronounced 'Jeth-art'), a shaft 7 or 8 feet long with a head shaped like an axe, that their war-cry, 'Jeddart's here', struck terror into many a stout heart. 'Jeddart justice' was a quick and convenient way of dealing with captives and other undesirables; it consisted of hanging a man first and trying him afterwards. Reminders of these restless days survive in the Jedburgh Callants' Festival, held each year in July, and even more in the Handba' Game, played through the streets at Candlemas (2nd February) between the 'uppies' and the 'doonies', those born above and below the site of the mercat cross.

The town has been almost entirely rebuilt since the disasters of the sixteenth century. Its prosperity revived with the introduction of woollen manufacture, and Jedburgh now has knitwear, rayon and tool-making factories. 'Jethart Snails' are not a local variety of mollusc, but a confection made from a recipe said to have been brought here by a prisoner during the Napoleonic Wars.

Facing the Market Place are the eighteenth-century New Gate, with the tall Town Steeple, built in 1755–61, and the former County Buildings, where Sir Walter Scott made his first appearance as an advocate in 1793, but rebuilt in 1812. Mary, Queen of Scots, came to Jedburgh to open the assizes in October, 1566, and lodged for a month in a sixteenth-century tower-house of characteristic Scottish type to the east of the High Street. Destroyed by the Earl of Surrey in 1523, it was rebuilt by the Kerrs of Ferniehirst and is now known as Mary, Queen of Scots, House. While proceeding here, Mary received news of the Earl of Bothwell, lying wounded at Hermitage Castle in far Liddesdale, over 20 miles away across rough and trackless country. In characteristic fashion, she hurried to visit him, but the effort of riding there and back in the short autumn day brought on a fever to which she nearly succumbed. The scandal that ensued was eagerly seized on by the queen's detractors, though in fact she was well accompanied on the journey and the proceedings at Hermitage were quite public. The house has been converted into a museum, with many interesting mementoes of the unhappy queen and her time. Upstairs are the queen's small bedroom and the room in which slept her four attendants (all named Mary).

Canongate leads east from the Market Place to the narrow medieval Auld Brig over the Jed Water. In Castlegate, south of the Market Place, Prince Charles Edward Stuart lodged at No. 11 in 1745, on his way over the Border. In Abbey Close, on the east of the street (leading to the abbey), Wordsworth and his sister Dorothy lodged in 1803 at No. 7 (a house recently rebuilt), during their Scottish tour, and they were visited here by Scott, who read to them part of his first long poem (then unpublished), *The Lay of the Last Minstrel*.

Jedburgh Abbey was founded in 1138 by David I as a priory for Augustinian canons from Beauvais (France), but was raised to the rank of abbey in 1152. Alexander III was married here in 1285 to Yolande, daughter of the Count of Dreux. The abbey suffered severely in the incessant Border wars; it was destroyed no less than seven times between 1300 and the punitive expedition of the Earl of Hertford in 1545. At the Dissolution, in 1560, it became the property of the Kerrs of Ferniehirst, and part of the nave was used as the parish church until a new church was built by the Marquess of Lothian in 1875.

The beautiful ruins, of a warm red sandstone, date mainly from the period between about 1152 and 1225. The west front of the church, built in 1180–1200, has a richly carved late-Norman doorway, and in the gable above is a fine wheel window, inserted in the fourteenth century. The long nave, severe but wholly satisfying, is the finest example in Scotland of Transitional Norman work, showing the transition from the round arches of the Norman style to the pointed arches of the early Gothic or First Pointed style. The graceful arcades have clustered piers, above which are the round arches of the triforium (literally the 'third stage'), each enclosing two pointed arches; and above this stage is the clerestory, with delicate pointed arches.

The crossing of the church, with its sturdy piers, was rebuilt after 1478 by Abbots Hall and Cranston, both of whom signed their work, but the tower it supports was rebuilt in 1508. At the end of the fifteenth-century north transept is the Lothian Chapel, containing monuments of the Kerrs, including an effigy of the eighth Marquess of Lothian carved in 1879 by G. F. Watts. Of the choir, the oldest work in the church, only two bays have survived, but these show a feature unique in Scotland; the massive round piers are carried up on the north side to support the triforium arches. Beyond are the remains of one bay of the presbytery, and on the south side is a fifteenth-century presbytery chapel, built by Abbot Hall.

At the east end of the south aisle is an exquisite late-Norman doorway whose detail work has been adversely affected by the weather, but happily its design has been reproduced in a modern doorway at the west end of the aisle. Both doorways admit to the foundations of the fourteenth-century conventual buildings, which slope down towards the river; and a splendid view is revealed from this side of the fine, unbroken ranges of windows in the nave. Near the west end of the church is a small museum containing sculptured stones, among them part of the 8th-century shrine of St Boisil of Old Melrose.

Castlegate ascends to the disused County Prison, built in 1823 on the site of Jedburgh Castle, which stood in a commanding position above the town. It became a royal residence, and Malcolm IV ('the Maiden') died here in 1165. Jedburgh was one of the five strongholds surrendered to England in 1174 as security for the ransom of William the Lion, captured outside Alnwick. The castle was completely demolished by order of the Scottish parliament in 1409 to preclude its further occupation by the invading English, to whom it often proved of more value than to the Scots themselves. The road past the prison leads up towards Dunion Hill (1092 feet) and Black Law (1110 feet), the twin summits of a long moorland range which commands a wide view extending from the Cheviot Hills on one hand to the Eildons and Ettrick Forest on the other.

In medieval times the country around the Jed Water comprised the great Forest of Jedworth, a district notorious for the wildness of its inhabitants, though undoubtedly these had some excuse in that they suffered more than any other of the Border Scots from the hands of the rapacious English invaders. The Capon Tree, a noble survivor of the forest, stands near Hundalee Mill, on the road for Carter Bar and the Border, which ascends the beautifully-wooded glen, crossing and recrossing the river.

Above the east bank of the Jed Water is Ferniehirst Castle, long a principal refuge of the Kerrs, ancestors of the Marquesses of Lothian. Built in 1476, it was captured after 'long skirmyshing' by the Earl of Surrey in 1523. The castle was devastated by the Earl of Hunsdon during the English invasion of 1570 and again in 1593 for the part played by the Kerrs in support of the Earl of Bothwell, when he became the third husband of Mary of Scots. After its restoration in 1598 Ferniehirst was called 'a charming example of a Scottish mansion of the period'. It is now a youth hostel, and on cold winter nights the hostellers (like the Kerrs of old) can gather round the huge fireplace in the fine great hall.

The road upstream follows the many windings of the 'crystal Jed', passing Old Jedward, the original site of Jedburgh. Beyond the hamlet of Camptown, where it crosses the river for the last time, the road leaves the narrow glen and climbs towards the lonely Border ridge. A road on the left, making for Pennymuir and the Kale Water (Chapter 11), passes north of the distinctive twin humps of Browndean (or Brundean) Laws, on the eastern of which (1358 feet) is a huge prehistoric mound or cairn over 40 feet in diameter. The main road finally zigzags up to Carter Bar (Chapter 4), where it crosses from Scotland into England, before descending into Redesdale on its way to Newcastle. Less than half a mile before reaching the summit, the Newcastle road is joined by a road from Hawick. This road descends westward at length over the flanks of Catcleuch Shin, at the northern end of the long ridge of Carter Fell (1900 feet), and drops down to the upper valley of the Jed Water at Southdean (pronounced 'Sou-den'), the Zedon of Froissart's *Chronicles*. Beside the river are the ruins of the church where James, Earl of Douglas, and other Scottish leaders assembled before the excursion into England that led to the Battle of Otterburn (Chapter 4). A service of commemoration is held each year on the second Sunday in August. On Southdean Law, to the north, are the double ramparts of an Early Iron Age fort.

The Hawick road crosses the Jed Water to the small village of Chesters, where the church, built in 1874, has a window commemorating James Thomson, the poet, author of *The Seasons* and *Rule, Britannia*, who spent his boyhood here in his father's manse, and attended the parish school before going on to Jedburgh. To the south the moorland ridges rise to the plantations of Wauchope Forest and beyond these to the great ridge carrying the Border from Carter Fell to Peel Fell (Chapter 3).

The main road, going on westward, is joined by the road from Liddesdale before descending steeply into the valley of the Rule Water at the hamlet of Bonchester Bridge. Near by is a village built by the Forestry Commission for the benefit of its workers in the state forest, like those in Redesdale and North Tynedale. The conspicuous Bonchester Hill (about 1000 feet), rising to the east, is ringed by the ramparts and ditches of a huge Iron Age fort. A delightful road descends the wooded valley for Bedrule (Chapter 11) and Jedburgh.

The road to Liddesdale ascends above the east side of the Rule Water at first, passing Wolfelee, where Prince Charles Edward Stuart and his ragged army camped on their way from Kelso to Carlisle. After staying one night in Jedburgh, where the Jacobites and their cause were ignored by the men, though the women flocked into the street to kiss the prince's hand, the insurgents passed into the Rule valley, from which they pushed on over the pass into Liddesdale.

The road climbs through the plantations of Wauchope Forest, part of the Border Forest Park (Chapter 3), to reach the summit of the pass at Note o' the Gate (about 1250 feet), where the trees now prevent any widespreading view. About a quarter-mile beyond the highest point the road emerges from the forest, and we have a view down towards the tributary streams of Liddesdale, with the Border heights to the left, extending from Peel Fell to the Larriston Fells. The moorland road descends into the narrow glen of the Dawston Burn to reach the farm of Saughtree (pronounced 'Saw-'), on the road from North Tynedale (Chapter 3) and in the angle between the burn and the Liddel Water, which rises near the Border and within half a mile of the source of the North Tyne.

Thorlieshope, a farm hidden among trees in a fold of the hills, east of Saughtree, was the home of Dandie Dinmont and his famous terriers in Scott's *Guy Mannering*, though the portrait of Dandie himself is said to have been taken from James Davison of Hyndlee, near the head of the Rule Water. Dawston Rig, the ridge above Saughtree to the north, is said to be that 'Daegsastan' where in A.D. 603 a great battle was fought between Ethelfrith, King of Northumbria, and Aidan, King of Strathclyde, as a result of which, says Bede, 'from that time no king of the Scots durst come into Britain to make war on the Angles to this day'. Riccarton Junction, beyond the ridge to the west of Saughtree, is a village built entirely to serve the needs of the railway, at the point where the Hawick-Carlisle line was joined by the line up North Tynedale. It could be reached only by footpath and railway, but now the railway is closed it is completely cut off from the outside world, except by path.

Our road descends Liddesdale, the long valley of the Liddel Water, which for about 8 miles above the Scots' Dike (Chapter 13) to the junction of the Kershope Burn divides Scotland from England. In its upper reaches the Liddel is a characteristic moorland burn, bounded by rolling hills which, though of no great height, have a character of their own, 'sinking their sides at once upon the river', in the words of J. G. Lockhart. Until towards the end of the eighteenth century, neither roads nor bridges had been provided in Liddesdale, and goods were still transported mainly on horseback. Sir Walter Scott, according to Lockhart, was the first man to drive a carriage into the dale, in 1800. This untamed country was formerly the terrain of the Armstrongs and the Elliots, hard-riding, reckless people who had a reputation for wild living even among the

Borderers themselves. The dale can have changed but little since Scott's day (even the once-intrusive railway has now practically disappeared), except along the eastern flanks beyond the Larriston Fells, where the landscape has taken on a new aspect in the hands of the Forestry Commission.

The road descending the dale passes opposite the farm of Larriston, on the site of a stronghold of the Elliots celebrated in a stirring ballad by James Hogg, the 'Ettrick Shepherd'. Above rise the lonely Larriston Fells (1678 feet), traversed by an old drove road from North Tynedale which crosses the Border at Bloody Bush (Chapter 3) and descends to the Liddel Water at Dinlabyre. Of Old Castleton, near the north end of Newcastleton Forest, nothing remains but a jumble of mounds and the churchyard. It originated as a settlement of the De Soulis family, hereditary King's Butlers of Scotland who lived at Liddel Castle farther downstream, on a high bank overlooking the river, but now likewise reduced to a few shapeless mounds.

The Liddesdale road turns to the left from a road which ascends the pleasant Hermitage Water towards Hawick. Beyond Newlands, a shooting-lodge of the Duke of Buccleuch (pronounced 'Buk-klú'), a road on the left goes on up the Water to Hermitage Castle, standing on a grassy plateau surrounded by wild green fells. One of the most formidable and unusual of Border strongholds, its design owes much to English influence. The first castle, built before the end of the thirteenth century, belonged to the De Bolbecks of Tyneside, who were succeeded by the De Soulis family, but as the possession of Liddesdale alternated between Scotland and England during the fourteenth century, the castle frequently changed hands. William de Soulis, called the 'Wizard', forfeited Hermitage in 1320 for conspiring against Robert Bruce, but in 1335 Edward Baliol granted the castle to Ralph Neville, an English supporter, from whom it was captured in 1338 by Sir William Douglas, the 'Knight of Liddesdale'. In 1342 Douglas starved his enemy, Sir Alexander Ramsay, to death here, though the prisoner is said to have eked out his existence for some seventeen days on the grains of corn that trickled through the roof of his dungeon from a granary overhead.

In about 1358 the property passed to the Dacres, another English family, and the oldest part of the existing castle was almost certainly built by them. It consists of a central courtyard enclosed by massive walls, with a spiral stairway on the north side, and has been attributed to John Lewyn, a master-mason from Durham who is known to have worked at Roxburgh Castle (in 1378) and at Coldingham Priory, in Berwickshire. By 1371 Hermitage had passed again to the Douglases, made Earls of Angus, and it is to them that the castle owes its present appearance. They embedded the Dacres' tower in a larger rectangular tower-house, and in about 1400 added four massive corner towers, strengthened by imposing connecting arches on the east and west sides which, more than anything, give the castle its unusual appearance. The south-west tower was extended in the fifteenth century, when the whole castle was surrounded by a corbelled parapet (since restored) with large corbel holes below for a timber platform.

In 1492 the Douglases, out of favour with the Crown, were forced to exchange Hermitage with the Hepburns, Earls of Bothwell, for Bothwell Castle, on the Clyde. The new owners proved equally untrustworthy and in 1540 the lordship of Liddesdale, with the castle, was annexed to the Crown. The Hepburns nevertheless mostly remained in possession, and in 1566 Queen Mary paid the hurried visit from Jedburgh to see the fourth Earl of Bothwell as he was lying wounded after a Border fray. In about 1594 the castle passed to the Scotts of Buccleuch and it played no further part in history.

The plateau on which Hermitage stands had been inhabited as early perhaps as the 6th century. It is known to have been the retreat of hermits from whom the castle subsequently took its name, and in about 1180 Walter de Bolbeck granted 'to Brother William of Mercheley' the hermitage in his 'waste' beside the Marching Burn, as the Hermitage Water was then known. The remains of a chapel, of the thirteenth or fourteenth century, still exist near the castle. Outside the enclosing wall, on the river side, is a long mound claimed to be the grave of the Cowt (i.e. colt) of Kielder, in North Tynedale, who was apparently renowned for his size and strength, and was consequently a thorn in the flesh of the Scottish Borderers. But while crossing the Hermitage Water below the chapel he was ambushed by the 'Wizard' Soulis and his followers, who kept him under water with their spears until he was drowned.

The road past the castle climbs westward over the hills and descends by the Carewoodrig Burn to the upper valley of the Ewes Water (Chapter 14). The Hawick road, crossing the Hermitage Water above

Newlands, ascends the tributary Whitrope Burn to the west of Nine Stane Rig, a long ridge that takes its name from a prehistoric circle of eight stones (one now fallen), the largest 6 feet high. Here the wicked Lord Soulis, the last of his line, was boiled alive in a pot by his exasperated followers, according to a ballad by John Leyden, though in reality he died in Dumbarton Castle, accused of treason. The road climbs up to Limekiln Edge (1182 feet), which commands a wild moorland view, before descending northward towards Teviotdale. Below the watershed and extending west below the Maiden Paps (1677 feet) is the line of the Catrail or Picts' Work Dike, a shallow ditch, difficult to distinguish in many places, with the excavated earth piled usually on the lower side of the slope across which it runs. This mysterious earthwork has been traced from the direction of Peel Fell, on the Border, north-west across Teviotdale to the Borthwick Water and beyond. Innumerable conjectures have been made about its origin and purpose. Some authorities have asserted that it was a boundary between the Britons of Strathclyde and the English of Northumbria, but even the derivation of the name is obscure. Professor Veitch found the nearest approach to the name in the Cornish 'cad,' battle, and 'treyle', to turn, i.e. a battle-turning, or defence work. The Hawick road descends to the Long Burn, then from Shankend goes on down to the steep glen of the Slitrig Water (Chapter 14).

The Liddesdale road goes southward through Newcastleton, a small town founded in 1793 by the Duke of Buccleuch as a weaving centre, and laid out on a regular plan, with a long main street interrupted by formal squares. Over the hills to the east extend the plantations of Newcastleton Forest, another part of the Border Forest Park. Beyond the farm of Mangerton, farther down the dale, are the remnants of a tower of the Armstrongs. Near the road is Millholm Cross, over 8 feet high, supposed to commemorate some unknown Armstrong who was buried here in the fourteenth century, and higher up lived John of the Syde ('a greater thief did never ride'), whose rescue from his enemies of Liddesdale by his cousins of Mangerton (the Laird's Jock and the Laird's Wat) is told in a lively ballad.

The Liddel Water is joined farther south by the Kershope Burn, which forms the boundary between Roxburghshire and Cumberland and separates Newcastleton Forest, on the north side, from Kershope Forest, the main Cumbrian section of the Border Forest Park. A road crosses the

Liddel (and the Border) to the hamlet of Kershopefoot, which has been enlarged by a settlement of forest workers like that at Bonchester Bridge. Little-used roads go on through the woodlands towards Bewcastle (Chapter 15) and Brampton.

The Liddesdale road crosses the Muir Burn, leaving Roxburghshire for Dumfriesshire. From the cross-roads in the scattered village of Harelaw we could cross the Liddel Water into Cumberland, then continue south of the river towards Longtown, skirting the grounds of Netherby Hall. The main road continues on the Scottish side of the river to cross the Esk and join the Hawick-Carlisle road at Canonbie (Chapter 14).

CHAPTER FOURTEEN

From Hawick to Eskdale

Hawick (pronounced 'Hoick') is an agricultural centre and industrial town finely situated at the confluence of the Slitrig Water with the Teviot, in the centre of Teviotdale. The largest town in Roxburghshire (and in the Border after Carlisle), it has an old-established livestock market and is the thriving seat of the Scottish manufacture of woollens, first introduced by Bailie John Hardie in 1771. Hawick is now noted for the knitting and weaving of tweeds and also produces yarn and hosiery, as well as chemicals for the textile industry. It has some good shops in its main street, and wears a look of general prosperity. As it contains few places of interest, it is usually overlooked by the tourist who 'picturesques it everywhere', and this is unfortunate, as the town has a definite atmosphere of its own, differing from that of other Border towns whose feet are still fixed firmly in the past.

The Kelso road (Chapter 11) joins that from Selkirk by a striking equestrian monument (sculptured by W. F. Beattie in 1914) to the 'callants' (i.e. youths) of Hawick, inscribed with their famous war-cry, 'Teribus, ye Teriodin', a phrase of obscure origin, though now vaguely linked with the Battle of Flodden Field. The Common Riding, or Riding of the Marches (i.e. the town boundaries), held early in June by the callants under their 'cornet', celebrates a skirmish at Hornshole Bridge, east of the town, in 1514, when the callants routed a party of English soldiers flushed with the victory of Flodden and captured their banner.

In the High Street are the imposing Town Buildings, the council offices of 1885, dominated by a Scottish baronial tower; and at the south end of the street is the Tower Hotel, incorporating a vaulted lower storey

177

of the Black Tower of Drumlanrig, a tower-house of the Douglases
rebuilt in the sixteenth century and the only survivor when the Earl of
Sussex burned the town in 1570. In about 1671 it passed to the Scotts of
Buccleuch, and in 1773 it became an inn. William and Dorothy
Wordsworth stayed here in 1803 on their Scottish tour. On a hill to the
south is St Mary's Church, rebuilt in 1763 and much restored since. It
replaces the church (first dedicated in 1214) in which Sir William
Douglas of Hermitage Castle seized Sir Alexander Ramsay, Sheriff of
Teviotdale and Warden of the East March, in 1342. Douglas, Lord of
Liddesdale, having cleared the English out of Teviotdale, claimed as a
right not only the wardenship of the Middle March but the keeping of
Roxburgh Castle, which Ramsay held as part of his office.

Howgate ascends from the church towards The Moat, or Mote, a hill
30 feet high and 300 feet round, perhaps the motte of a Norman castle
and later the meeting-place of the court of the manor. From it a fine view
is revealed of the junction of the glen of the Slitrig Water with that of the
Teviot and of the green hills that protrude around the town. On Kaim
Law (777 feet), a ridge about a mile out of Hawick, east of the road to
Liddesdale (Chapter 13), are the remains of an elongated prehistoric fort,
about 360 feet long.

The road from Hawick towards the head of Teviotdale (and Carlisle)
keeps to the south side of the Teviot at first. On the other side of the
rushing, amber-hued river is an attractive public park enclosing Wilton
Lodge, now housing a museum of old Hawick and its neighbourhood.
The collections illustrate prehistory and natural history, Border life and
crafts, and the knitwear industry, and include the original stockinger's
handframe introduced by John Hardie.

Higher up is the enticing entrance to the glen of the Borthwick Water,
more pastoral than most upland valleys in the Border. Opposite, above
the Teviot, is Goldielands (formerly Gaudylands), a farmhouse em-
bodying a tower-house of the Scotts, the last of whom is reputed to have
been hanged over his own gateway because of his cattle-lifting propen-
sities. On the other side of the dale, farther on, is Branxholm (or
Branksome) Tower, the principal setting of *The Lay of the Last Minstrel*,
though 'nine-and-twenty knights of fame' never 'hung their shields' in this
hall, and never were attended by 'nine-and-twenty squires of name' and
'nine-and-twenty yeomen tall'. There is not the room for them, and there

was even less room in the tower's predecessor, which stood at the period when the poem was set. Branxholm was a stronghold of the Scotts of Buccleuch, who were here from 1420 on, but it was blown up by the English in 1570, when Buccleuch stood loyal to the unlucky Mary of Scots, after which the older parts of the present house, the tower and the south front (since restored) were built.

The dale adopts a more open and moorland nature as the road goes on to the hamlet of Teviothead (*not* the head of the Teviot, which rises some 7 miles farther up). In the old churchyard is a memorial to Johnny Armstrong of Gilnockie (in Eskdale), a famous reiver who 'rode ever with twenty-four able gentlemen well horsed; yet he never molested any Scottishman'. In the sixteenth century the Armstrongs of Liddesdale and Eskdale were the most formidable freebooters in the Border country. In 1530, in a campaign against the lawlessness of the Border, James V arrested many of the more powerful lairds, hanging some but pardoning others who gave sureties for good behaviour. Johnny Armstrong, accompanied by 40 of his followers, came to meet the king at Caerlanrig, on the ridge beyond the church at Teviothead, either of his own volition or under the persuasion of the king, it is not clear which. He certainly came with the hope of making peace, but his excuse that he levied blackmail on the king's enemies across the Border was precisely that mode of behaviour to which the king objected, and he was summarily hanged.

Also buried in Teviothead churchyard is Henry Scott Riddell, the song-writer, author of *Scotland Yet*, who was born at Sorbie in Wigtownshire in 1798, but came here to be minister of the parish. He died in 1870 and is commemorated by a conspicuous cairn on the hill above the dale to the north-east. A farm road goes on towards the head reaches of the Teviot, which rises below White Hope Edge (1560 feet), in lonely trackless country extending westward to the glen of the White Esk.

At Teviothead the road to Carlisle leaves the main valley and climbs beside the tributary Frostlie Burn, between steep grassy hills, to reach the watershed (853 feet) between the Teviot and the Esk. Beyond, at the Mosspaul Inn, on the site of an old posting-station, the road leaves Roxburghshire for Dumfriesshire. It then descends rapidly through a twisting steep-sided defile, hemmed in by the green flanks of the bare hills, while now and again, up some tributary burn, a view opens to a lonely corrie

secreted among the round-backed clustered heights. Below one of these
side glens, that of the Carewoodrig Burn, up which runs a wild road that
crosses to Hermitage Castle (Chapter 13) and Liddesdale, the defile
suddenly spreads out into the long and beautiful valley of the Ewes
Water, one of the chief tributaries of the Dumfriesshire Esk, its level
strath enriched by pastures, while pine woods climb the lower slopes of
the hillsides opposite. Among the upland dales of the Border, this is one
of the finest.

The road from Hawick, crossing the Meikledale Burn, one of the
larger tributaries, runs below Brieryshaw Hill, a promontory of Stake
Hill (1349 feet), with the large double ramparts and ditch of an Iron Age
fort. The Ewes Water flows into the Esk at Langholm, a prosperous
small town in a very lovely setting. It makes tweeds (the woollen mills,
happily, are fairly unobtrusive) and is noted as an angling centre. In 1455
at Langholm (or Arkinholm, as it was then called) was fought the first of
the decisive battles which resulted in the powerful and ambitious house of
Douglas being finally crushed by the Stewarts.

Facing the small cobbled market place, at the south end of the narrow
High Street, is the Town Hall of 1811. On the wall is a plaque to
William Julius Mickle, translator of *The Lusiad* of the sixteenth-century
Portuguese poet Camoens, and the author of the ballad of *Cumnor Hall*
(which suggested to Scott the writing of *Kenilworth*) and 'There's nae
luck aboot the hoose'. He was born in the town in 1734, the son of the
minister. Langholm, like Hawick, still celebrates its Common Riding, and
the event takes place here on the last Friday in July. The proclamation at
the 'crying of the fair' reminds potential disturbers of the peace of the
penalty that 'they shall sit down on their bare knees and pray seven times
for the King, and thrice for the Muckle Laird o' Ralton'. The Laird was
an illegitimate son of Charles II, but his connection with Langholm is
obscure.

Smooth green hills rise all round the town and offer excellent views
over the twin valleys of the Esk and the Ewes Water. The heather-
covered Whita Hill (1163 feet), to the east, is surmounted by a tall
obelisk commemorating Major-General Sir John Malcolm, the Indian ad-
ministrator, the best known of the four brother 'Knights of Eskdale', who
was born in 1769 at Burnfoot, 3 miles up the Esk. From the hill we have
an exceptionally wide prospect: to the Pennines, to Skiddaw in the Lake

District, to the shining Solway Firth and the mouths of its many feeders, to the solitary Criffel and the hills about the heads of Nithsdale and Annandale, and to the heights bounding the upper reaches of Eskdale and Liddesdale.

The course of the Esk for several miles below Langholm can stake a high claim to be among the most charming in the Border, rivalling even some reaches of the noble Tweed, though the Esk is on a smaller scale. In the great days of coaching, this section of the highway between Edinburgh and London had the reputation of being the most attractive in the whole journey. The road, after crossing the Esk at Skipper's Bridge, keeps close to the west bank of the broad river, which rushes along through a rocky glen luxuriantly filled with trees. On a green haugh in a bend of the Esk stands Holehouse or Hollows Tower, a pele of the Armstrongs, built after 1518 and now roofless. Gilnockie Bridge, just below, where the road re-crosses the river, is built of stones taken from the vanished Gilnockie Tower, the stronghold of that Johny Armstrong hanged at Teviothead.

On a fine reach of the Esk, below its exit from the narrow part of the glen, is Canonbie, now a pleasant village, with an old coaching inn (the Cross Keys), but once a place of some importance. The church, on the other side of the river, which flows between red sandstone cliffs, was built in 1822 by William Atkinson, the architect of Sir Walter Scott's Abbotsford. No fragment now remains of the twelfth-century Augustinian priory that stood on this bank, on the neck of the isthmus formed by the curving Liddel Water before it joins the major river. In later days a cell of Jedburgh Abbey, it was possibly demolished by the English following their crushing defeat of the Scots on Solway Moss in 1542, after which, like many another ruin, it would be used extensively as a quarry for building stones.

Beyond the point where the Esk and the Liddel meet, the Border between Scotland and England, which has come down through Liddesdale (Chapter 13), leaves the river for the Scots' Dike, the earthwork, nearly $3\frac{1}{2}$ miles long, constructed across country west to the River Sark after the final settlement of the line of the Border in 1552. The boundary now appears as a low mound with traces of a shallow ditch on each side, running through the middle of a long plantation. On either side of the Dike extended the 'Debatable Land,' a tract mostly of level and now fertile country that was in constant dispute between the contending nations until the settlement of the Border line. It was bounded by the Esk and the Sark, but reached northward to Windy Edge, west of Kershopefoot.

Among the broad meadows through which winds the Esk is the solitary church of Kirkandrews, rebuilt in 1776 and formerly serving perhaps the largest parish in Cumberland. This extended for 20 miles up the southern sides of the Liddel Water and the Kershope Burn, though it was only 3 or 4 miles broad. Downstream from the church is Kirkandrews Tower, a well-restored sixteenth-century pele, of characteristically Scottish type, that belonged to the Graham family. On the other side of the river is the large and beautifully-wooded park that encloses Netherby Hall, a fifteenth-century tower which was the home since 1620 of the Grahams, whose heiress was carried off by the young Lochinvar in Scott's stirring ballad, in *Marmion*. The tower was incorporated in a much larger house built in 1833 by William Burn. Close by is the site of a Roman fort with the rich name of *Castra Exploratorum*; it stood on a road that ran from Carlisle towards the Clyde valley but made a wide detour to avoid the marshy levels bounding the Solway Firth.

The Grahams, whose pele towers were once scattered throughout the length of the Debatable Land, had an evil reputation in the sixteenth century, though they were probably no worse than other families at that time in the lawless, hard-living Border. But they had the misfortune to fall foul of the authorities and particularly of Lord Scrope, the English Warden of the West March (who believed them to have been involved in the rescue of Kinmont Willie from Carlisle Castle), and when James VI also became king of England he had them outlawed, the women and children turned from their homes and the men deported to Holland and Ireland. Though many of the Grahams later returned to the Border, it was to find their towers destroyed or pillaged, their families scattered and their power gone.

High above the Liddel Water, and half a mile upstream from its junction with the Esk, in a commanding position, are the earthworks of Liddel Strength (sometimes called Liddel Mote). These are the sole remains of a once-massive castle which was enclosed by a deep ditch. Referred to as the 'Piel of Ledel' in 1320, it was probably built before either Hermitage Castle or Liddel Castle, farther upstream, but it was demolished by David II during his ill-fated incursion into England in 1346.

The Carlisle road crosses the broadening Esk to Longtown, a former market town laid out on a regular plan, with wide streets, in the late eighteenth century. It began to decline in importance after the close of the coaching era and now bears an atmosphere of decay that is only accentuated by the vast amount of heavy road traffic that hurries through the town, destroying its peace. The parish church, built of red sandstone in 1609 in the Gothic style, is at Arthuret, three-quarters of a mile south in the town, to the west of the uninteresting road to Carlisle.

The road to the west from the Esk bridge skirts the south side of Solway Moss, now a region of heather and pines, but once a quaking bog. In 1542 James V, returning from England with 10,000 Scots, was surprised here and roundly defeated by a much smaller force under Sir Thomas Wharton, a catastrophe that is said to have hastened the king's death. The Moss is part of an extensive tract of flat land stretching down to the shores of the Solway Firth, round the estuaries of the Esk, the Lyne and the Eden. A vast wilderness until the mid-eighteenth century, when it was drained and cultivated, this became one of the most productive areas in the Border before the Government in 1914 commandered a large area of land for munition factories and other works.

The road from Longtown crosses the small River Sark, part of the boundary since 1552, and re-enters Scotland. The first place on the Scottish side, three-quarters of a mile from the Border, is Gretna Green, once the goal of runaway couples from England intent on taking advantage of the Scottish law, under which they could be married by making a simple declaration before two witnesses. But from 1856 on, Scottish law required a residential qualification of three weeks for one of the couple, and in 1940 marriage 'by declaration' became illegal. The wedding anvil and other curios are shown in the famous smithy, beside the Longtown road, where the blacksmith performed the ceremony and witnesses were always on hand. The ceremonies also took place in local inns, at the eighteenth-century Gretna Hall (south of the smithy, near the Carlisle road) and at the Sark Toll-House, established in 1830, where the main road to Carlisle crosses the Sark into England.

CHAPTER FIFTEEN

To Carlisle and the Solway Firth

Between the Liddel Water, descending through Liddesdale (Chapter 13), and the line of Hadrian's Wall extends a vast tract of unknown country forming the triangular northern corner of Cumberland. It consists largely of moorland and rough grassland (though the plantations of Kershope Forest now fill the apex of the triangle) and has many small farms but few villages or places of interest. This region is mostly drained by the feeders of the Irthing, a large tributary of the Eden (which flows past Carlisle), and the two branches of the Lyne, which joins the Esk before this river enters the Solway Firth.

Almost in the middle of this region is one place of absorbing interest whose history goes back to Roman times: Bewcastle. It can be reached by round-about roads from Canonbie and Liddesdale, on the west, and from Brampton and Gilsland, to the south. From Birdoswald, on Hadrian's Wall (Chapter 2), a Roman road, sometimes called the Maiden Way, reached out across the open moors to an outlying fort here of unknown name. Along this 'rugged causeway' the hero of *Guy Mannering* rode with Dandie Dinmont towards Liddesdale, after their encounter with the freebooters from Mumps Ha'. This route still makes an exhilarating walk, though today there are scant signs of the old road.

The small village of Bewcastle is peacefully situated on the Kirk Beck, a tributary of the White Lyne, among the folds of the low grey-brown hills that rise towards Sighty Crag (1701 feet) and Christianbury Crag (1598 feet), the highest points of the rather indeterminate country on the Northumberland boundary, where the extension of the Pennines beyond the Tyne Gap meets the range of Border hills. These trackless and

desolate wastes were notorious for the activities of moss-troopers before
the Union, and Bewcastle itself suffered frequently through predatory
raids across the Border.

The ramparts which are now the only sign of the Roman fort enclose
the church, mainly rebuilt in 1792, and the ruins of a castle, 'Beuth's
Castle,' first built before the Normans came and completely rebuilt in
about 1300. This was an important outpost during the troublous times of
the Tudor period, but the castle was destroyed in the Civil War. In the
churchyard is the most interesting relic at Bewcastle, an outstanding
Anglian cross, 14½ feet high, carved from grey stone quarried in the
neighbourhood. It was once higher, but the top was removed by Belted
Will Howard of Naworth and sent to William Camden, the antiquary,
and it has since disappeared. The cross has been dated to the late 7th century, after the victory of Romish ideas at the great Synod at Whitby,
when sculptors came to Britain from Italy and taught the native stone-
carvers. Like the cross at Ruthwell in Dumfriesshire, the work of the same
school, it shows an interesting intermingling of Roman and Celtic ideas.
The conception of a tall cross is Celtic in origin, a development of the simple megalith, but the sculpture is of pure Italian inspiration. On each of
the four sides of the cross are elaborate carvings, including the earliest
representation of the figure of Christ to be found in Britain, and on three
sides are Runic inscriptions whose meaning is still a mystery to the antiquary.

The road to the south from Bewcastle crosses the moors to Banks
(Chapter 2), on Hadrian's Wall. From here a steep descent leads into the
delightful broad green valley of the Irthing for Lanercost Priory
(pronounced 'Lan-ner-'). Founded in about 1166 for Augustinian canons
by Robert de Vaux, the priory is built of that warm red sandstone
characteristic of this part of Cumberland; many of the stones, in fact,
came from the Roman wall. It was often 'visited' by the Scots, including
Wallace and Bruce; and Edward I stayed here on his expeditions into
Scotland in 1280 and 1300, and again in 1307, before his fatal journey
to the shores of the Solway Firth.

The priory is charmingly situated on the strath, and as one enters
through the low-arched thirteenth-century gateway, the west front of the
church, an exquisite example of Early English architecture, is in full view.
High up in the gable is a beautiful figure of St Mary Magdalen, sculp-

tured in about 1270; it bears a strong resemblance to parts of the magnificent Angel Choir of Lincoln Cathedral and may well be the work of a sculptor from Lincoln. The great west door leads directly into the fine Early English nave, completed by about 1220, but restored in 1740 for use as the parish church. The new wall then provided below the west arch of the crossing has windows with fragments of sixteenth-century glass showing the arms of Thomas Dacre of Naworth. The choir and transepts beyond, of about 1200, remain in ruins, and the richly-sculptured fifteenth-to-sixteenth-century tombs of the Dacres here contrast rather incongruously with the quiet dignity of the church.

Around the cloister at Lanercost survive parts of the domestic buildings of the priory, including the Cellarium (a storehouse below the Refectory), with a vaulted ceiling, and the Prior's House, which with the rest of the western range of building was converted after the Dissolution into a private dwelling for the Dacres. The thirteenth-century east end of the vicarage (near the west door) was once the guest house of the canons; its west end dates from the sixteenth century.

The Irthing is crossed at Lanercost by a handsome medieval bridge of one arch, supplemented by a plain new bridge. On the south side of the valley extends the beautifully wooded park of Naworth Castle (pronounced 'Nah-'). The castle, one of the most interesting strongholds in the Border, was fortified in about 1335, when Ranulph Dacre was granted 'licence to crenellate' by Edward III. A pele tower of obscure origin stood on the site, and Dacre rebuilt this and added a wall enclosing a courtyard on the south, the other sides being guarded effectively by two steep little valleys. The castle was extended in about 1520 by Thomas Dacre, a Lord Warden of the West March who made himself prominent on Flodden Field. He strengthened the Dacre tower, built another tower (now known as Lord William's) with the Great Hall, 120 feet long, and added an outer bailey defended by a gatehouse, which still bears his crest and initials and the family motto, *Fort en loyauté*.

In 1577 Naworth passed from the Dacres to the powerful Howards by the marriage of 'Bess of the Braid Apron', so called from the extent of the estates that formed her dowry, to Lord William Howard, third son of the Duke of Norfolk. Only 14 years of age at the time of his wedding, Howard lived at Naworth for 40 years, during which time he converted the castle into a splendid Jacobean dwelling house. He rearranged the apartments, building the Long Gallery in the thickness of the wall, and he laid out a walled garden on the southern side. Lord William Howard was known along the Border as 'Belted Will', and he comes into *The Lay of the Last Minstrel*, though Scott has drawn him in the character of a rough feudal lord of an earlier period. In reality he was one of the first country gentlemen of the North, a scholar and a writer, collecting books and manuscripts, taking an interest in antiquities, and managing his estates with scrupulous care. He was among the foremost in using his powerful influence to reduce the Border to order after the Union of the Crowns. Howard's grandson took the field as one of Cromwell's colonels and became a Commissioner for the Northern Counties. For his services concerning the restoration of Charles II in 1660 he was created Earl of Carlisle, and the castle remains the property of his descendants.

In 1844 Naworth was ravaged by a fire which destroyed nearly all the interior of the main block, apart from Lord William's Tower, this being saved by an intervening iron-bound door introduced by Lord William himself. A careful restoration was carried out by Anthony Salvin, who in 1881 added a new wing on the north. The Great Hall now has a rich ceiling of about 1350 brought from Kirkoswald Castle, in the Eden valley. From the drive up to the main gate on the Brampton road we have a grand retrospect over Naworth to the distant hills of Dumfriesshire.

The park is skirted on the south by the Military Road, which comes over moorland from Greenhead (Chapter 2) and continues west to Brampton, an old-world market town built partly of the Cumbrian red sandstone. The road enters the town by The Sands, an open space where the fairs were once held, passing close to a huge conical hill, over 130 feet high, now covered by trees. If this were the motte of a castle, there is no evidence of a bailey. The main street runs south of and roughly parallel to the Carlisle road, and the two are joined by a tortuous lane which contains the house where Prince Charles Edward lodged in 1745, receiving the mayor and corporation of Carlisle when on their knees they surrendered the keys of the city.

Brampton has a market charter dating from the thirteenth century, and at the east end of the irregular main street is the cobbled Market Place, with the octagonal Moot Hall of 1817, which has unusual iron stocks outside. The Parish Church, to the west, rebuilt in 1878, is the only church by Philip Webb, friend of the pre-Raphaelites. It has seven windows full of glowing stained glass by William Morris (for whom Webb built the famous Red House at Bexley Heath, in Kent) and Sir Edward Burne-Jones.

The charm of Brampton's countryside for me goes back to boyhood days spent camping on the hills of gorse and sweet grass above the town to the south (the foothills of the Pennines) and exploring the Gelt Woods for the Written Rock, the inscription of a Roman workman carved in A.D. 207 while quarrying stone for the Wall. The main Carlisle road crosses the Gelt below the woods and goes on to Warwick Bridge, a village with woollen manufactures, beyond which the road crosses a bold sweep of the Eden on a fine bridge of 1837 by John Dobson. The church of Warwick, on the west bank, was rebuilt in about 1870, but incorporates a Norman tower arch and apse, with rare pilasters forming arched recesses.

Carlisle (the accent is on the second syllable), the county and assize town of Cumberland (and now of the new county of Cumbria), is by far the largest town near the Border and one of the most historic places in Britain. A settlement was first established here because of the existence of a low sandstone bluff (now occupied by the cathedral and the castle) between two small tributaries of the Eden, the Caldew and Petteril. On this site, in A.D. 79, Agricola chose to build a fort which subsequently grew into the important town and administrative centre of *Luguvalium*. Excavations of 1973–74, north of the cathedral, have revealed what appear to be the remains of barracks of Agricola's time. The course of Hadrian's Wall runs through the suburb of Stanwix (pronounced 'Stanix'), on the north side of the Eden, where the crossing of the broad river was controlled by the fort of *Petriana*, the largest on the Wall.

The Saxon settlement which followed the Roman town was given in 945 to Malcolm I of Scotland, but in 1092 the town was refounded by William Rufus, who ordered it to be fortified as a defence against the Scots. An Augustinian priory was founded in the following year, and in 1133 its church became the seat of a bishop. As a significant Border fortress, Carlisle was frequently attacked by the Scots; it was in their hands from about 1135 until about 1157, and David I, who is credited with beginning a new castle, died here in 1153. Carlisle later became a thriving city (the 'merrie Carlisle' of many a Border ballad) and when the defence of the frontier was organised in the three Marches, it was selected as the headquarters of the Warden of the West March.

The castle comprises three wards or baileys, if the open space outside the sturdy thirteenth-century Outer Gatehouse, or De Ireby's Tower, can be called a bailey; it was protected on the south only by a ditch (since filled in) and seems never to have been seriously defended. The two main baileys are separated by a mid-fourteenth-century wall, breached through the Inner Gatehouse or Captain's Tower. Over the archway to this, on the inner face, are a series of cusped trefoils, an unusual feature in military architecture. The gatehouse was strengthened in the sixteenth century by Stephen the Almain, a German engineer, who increased the width of the rampart to provide space for cannon, and at the same time added a half-moon battery on the outer side, encroaching on the ditch here. In the Inner Ward is the museum of the King's Own Royal Border Regiment, whose barracks and training ground now occupy most of the Outer Bailey.

The small Inner Ward is further restricted by the massive Norman keep, probably built in about 1170 by Henry II, who had first arrived in the city in 1156 to receive homage from Malcolm IV of Scotland. The keep has architectural affinities with others of the period. The foundations are still to be seen of a forebuilding through which the keep was originally entered on the first floor, as at Newcastle, where the keep was built in 1172. At Carlisle the keep is divided into two by a wall extending the full height of the building, as in the White Tower of London; and the smoke from the fireplace of the Great Hall, on the first floor, was allowed to escape through slits in the wall, as at Portchester (Hampshire), begun in about 1160, instead of by a chimney.

During the Wars of the Roses, prisoners were confined in the castle, and the walls of a room on the second floor of the keep are carved with their curious emblems. A decorative fourteenth-century stair-tower in the Inner Ward, known as Queen Mary's Tower, recalls that the Queen of Scots took refuge here in 1568 (after her defeat at the Battle of Langside, near Glasgow), relying on the clemency of Elizabeth I to obtain her liberty. But after two months imprisonment in the castle the unhappy queen was transferred to Bolton Castle in Wensleydale and never regained her freedom.

During the Civil War, Carlisle withstood for nearly nine months a siege by the Parliamentary Scots under General Leslie, who replied to its surrender in 1645 by demolishing the west end of the cathedral to repair the castle and the city walls. In 1745 Prince Charles Edward Stuart rode into Carlisle, mounted in triumph on a milk-white horse and preceded by the 'hundred pipers' of the famous Jacobite song, but a few weeks later the city surrendered again to the Duke of Cumberland. After the suppression of the rising, the heads of several of the defeated leaders were set up on the city walls. Some 300 prisoners were detained in the cathedral (where further damage was done) and in the castle, as described by Scott in *Waverley*. One of these was Major Macdonald of Keppoch, agreed to have been the prototype of Fergus MacIvor in the novel.

The most stirring episode in the annals of Carlisle is the rescue in 1596 of Kinmont Willie, the subject of a well-known ballad. The Wardens of the West March had declared, as was usual, a day of truce following one of their periodical meetings, and William Armstrong, of the notorious family of moss-troopers, was riding quietly home through Liddesdale when he was surprised by an English force and carried off to Carlisle Castle, there to be confined in a dungeon in the west wall. The Scots, smarting under this unjustifiable insult, and unable to obtain Kinmont's release through the intervention of the higher authorities, themselves determined on his rescue. Led by Sir Walter Scott of Buccleuch, the Keeper of Liddesdale and the 'bold Buccleuch' of the ballad, they set out on a dark night, with a heavy rain falling and a mist beginning to rise from the flats around the city, forded the swollen Eden and forced their way into the castle through a postern door (still to be seen) in the west wall. Buccleuch divided his followers into two parts, one lying between the castle and the city, to avoid any possibility of attack in the rear, while the other sought out Kinmont's dungeon, making as much clamour as possible 'to terrifie both castell and toune by ane imaginatioun of a greater force'. The door was wrenched open and Kinmont, though secured by chains, was hoisted bodily on to the back of a powerful Borderer called Red Rowan. The attackers did not stop until they had crossed both Eden and Esk, when they knocked up a smith to remove the captive's chains. Lord Scrope, the English Warden of the March, though possessed of an adequate force, all this time neither attacked nor pursued the Scots. Perhaps he was loath to incriminate himself further by enforcing that breach of Border law to which he had been a partner.

Despite its long and stormy chronicle, Carlisle is a city mainly of modern aspect, though it has not lost entirely its Border flavour. Always a flourishing agricultural centre, it grew in the nineteenth century to be an important railway junction, on the main line from London and Manchester to Glasgow and Edinburgh by the 'West Coast' route. Carlisle still has large marshalling yards, and the railway has brought numerous industries; the town now has many engineering works (making cranes, dockyard appliances etc.), as well as metal works and textile mills, and it makes biscuits, confectionery and footwear.

From Court Square, in front of the Citadel Station, English Street passes between the two immense round towers of the County Buildings and the Court House, rebuilt in 1807–11 by Thomas Telford and Sir Robert Smirke, but possibly incorporating some walls of the Citadel founded in 1541 by Henry VIII. They stand near the site of the Englishgate (or Botchergate), one of the three gates in the walls which completed the city's defences. (The others, the Rickergate or Scotchgate, towards the Eden, and the Irishgate, east of the Caldew Bridge, have also disappeared.)

English Street leads north to the triangular Market Place, with the Market Cross, put up in 1682 and remarkable for its four-faced sundial, and the picturesque Town Hall, rebuilt in 1717. The prisoners taken during the 1745 rebellion faced their trial here. Behind the Town Hall is the picturesque St Alban's Row, and next to it is the Redness Hall, or Guildhall, the meeting place of the medieval trade guilds, partly of the fourteenth century and the only timber-framed building in the city. In Castle Street, which leads past the impressive east end of the cathedral, Charlotte Charpentier stayed at No. 81 before her marriage to Walter Scott in the cathedral in 1797.

Carlisle Cathedral, originally the church of the Augustinian priory founded in 1093, was mostly completed by 1123 and became the only Augustinian church in England to be the seat of a bishop. It must have been one of the most imposing cathedrals before the six west bays of the nave were demolished in 1645 by Leslie's Scots. This destruction made Carlisle the smallest cathedral in England (with the exception of Oxford) and as a result it has been one of the least regarded. This is indeed unfortunate, as it has many features of unusual interest and beauty.

The two remaining bays of the nave (now a memorial chapel of the Border Regiment) are characteristic Norman work of the twelfth century. The distortion of the arcades above the massive piers is the result of the settlement of the foundations during building. The south transept is also Norman (in its west wall is a Runic inscription, probably of the eleventh century), but the north transept was rebuilt in the Decorated style of architecture in 1390 by Bishop Strickland. Rebuilding of the beautiful choir, with Early English arcades and vaulted aisles, was begun in about 1225, but it was gutted by fire in 1292, after which the triforium and clerestory were rebuilt by Bishop Halton. The piers were also replaced (before 1324) and their capitals have interesting carvings depicting the Employments of the Months, a favourite medieval subject.

The exquisite late-Decorated east window, the glory of the cathedral, is 51 feet high and has stained glass of 1380–84 in the tracery showing the Last Judgement. The stalls, with carved misericords (or brackets under the seats), were installed in 1413–33, and their backs were painted between 1484 and 1507 with the Apostles and legendary scenes from the lives of saints. The delicate screenwork of St Catherine's Chapel, in the south choir aisle, dates from about 1500; on the north of the choir is a Renaissance screen introduced in 1542 by Prior Lancelot Salkeld. The magnificent sixteenth-century Flemish pulpit was brought here in 1964 from the church of Cockayne Hatley, in Bedfordshire.

Salkeld was the last to hold the office of prior, and when the see was refounded by Henry VIII after the dissolution of the priory in 1540, he became the first dean. The nave was subsequently used as the parish church until its destruction. The Close, on the south of the cathedral, was previously surrounded by the domestic buildings of the priory, but of these practically the only survivals are the Refectory, rebuilt in 1482 and now the chapter library, and the great Gatehouse at the west end, built in 1527.

Castle Street goes on north from the cathedral past the entrance to Tullie House, a distinguished mansion of 1689, now containing the City Museum, which has an exceptionally fine collection of Roman antiquities from Cumberland and especially from Hadrian's Wall, as well as exhibits of local history from Viking times onward and of the natural history of the Lakeland counties. In the art gallery upstairs are nineteenth- and twentieth-century paintings. The Roman collection is rivalled only by those at Chesters and in the Museum of Antiquities in Newcastle University. It is in such carefully-arranged museums, even more than along the Wall, that we can obtain the best impressions of life under the Romans.

The green in front of the castle is bounded by two sections of the city wall, begun in the thirteenth century. From here Finkle Street descends towards the distinctive Civic Centre, built in 1964 by Charles B. Pearson, Son & Partners, with an octagonal council chamber. Lowther Street leads south back towards Court Square, passing the Congregational Church of 1843, replacing that in Annetwell Street of which Thomas Woodrow, grandfather of President Woodrow Wilson, was minister from 1820 to 1835. In the other direction, Eden Bridge, built by Sir Robert Smirke in 1815 (but since widened), crosses the river to the residential suburb of Stanwix. The site of *Petriana* is just to the right beyond the bridge, but nothing is to be seen above the ground.

A pathway south of the bridge follows the north wall of the castle, which has some heavy buttresses of the twelfth century. Bitts Park farther north, bounded by the Eden, is the setting for the County Agricultural Show, in June. Turning south, the path passes the postern gate in the west wall of the castle through which the 'bold Buccleuch' entered to rescue Kinmont Willie. Beyond Annetwell Street, which leads to the Caldew Bridge, a street named West Walls continues past the Deanery, formerly the Prior's House (incorporating a sixteenth-century pele), towards St Cuthbert's Church, one of the many in the North dedicated to the bishop-hermit, but rebuilt in 1778. Farther on is a restored tithe-barn of about 1490, built by Prior Gondibour, with another section of the city wall close by.

From the Caldew Bridge, roads run westward on the south side of the Eden, picking up the line of Hadrian's Wall before reaching Burgh-by-Sands (pronounced 'Bruff'). The restored church, which stands within the fort of *Aballava*, has a fortified tower, probably of the fourteenth century, an Early English arcade, built of Roman stones, and an unusual vestry, at the east end of the chancel. In the Solway marshes, over a mile north, is a monument marking the place where Edward I died in 1307, while on his way to make another attempt to quell the Scots under Robert Bruce.

The road westward, following the course of the Wall (nothing of which is to be seen), skirts Burgh Marsh to Drumburgh (also '-bruff'), on the Solway Firth, with the site of the smallest fort ($\frac{3}{4}$-acre) on Hadrian's Wall, possibly named *Congavata*. The Castle (now a farmhouse) was in fact a manor house built in the early sixteenth century, with stones from the Wall. The road goes through Port Carlisle, a small port which was developed after 1819 but declined after the building of the railway from Carlisle to Silloth, near the mouth of the estuary.

Bowness-on-Solway (the 'Bow-' is pronounced as in 'now') has a church, basically Early English (though restored in 1892), built with Roman stones and with a late-Norman font-bowl. It stands within the earthworks that mark the fort of *Maia* (about $5\frac{1}{2}$ acres), at the western end of Hadrian's Wall and commanding perhaps the lowest possible ford over the Solway. Excavations so far carried out have shown that the fort was of turf and timber in the 1st and 2nd centuries, but was then rebuilt in stone. It has long been known that the Wall defences were supplemented by a series of small forts extending down the shore of the Solway towards Maryport, but recent excavations to the west of Bowness have revealed that the defences were more complicated than previously thought. Systems of ditches and palisades, some indicating 1st- and 2nd-century occupation, have been discovered at Biglands and Car-durnock, to the west, but further excavation is required before the com-plete pattern of the defences becomes clear.

The Solway Firth is a wide estuary about 40 miles long formed mainly by the combined outflow of the Nith, the Annan, the Sark, the Esk and the Eden. Its sands are unsafe for bathing, but salmon fishing is still carried on from Bowness, using the old Norse 'haaf net', a reminder that the coast of Cumberland was settled by invaders from Norway. The firth is notorious for its rapidly-flowing tides, which sometimes form a bore up to 4 feet high, and as Darsie Latimer was cautioned in Scott's *Red gauntlet*, 'he that dreams on the bed of the Solway may wake in the next world'.

Here, on the flat shores of the Solway, at the farthest extremity of Hadrian's Wall and facing across the firth into Scotland, as the 'auld enemy' did for centuries, we leave the Border Country. It is a far cry, not only in distance but in spirit, to the great castles of Warkworth, Alnwick and Bamburgh, to the noble abbey ruins of Jedburgh, Dryburgh and Melrose, to the early Christian associations of Hexham and Lindisfarne, to old-world towns such as Berwick and Kelso, to the home of the greatest Borderer at Abbotsford, to the exhilarating heights of the Cheviot Hills, to the long dales full of history and romance, those of Teviot, Esk and Liddel on one side, of Coquet, Rede and Tyne on the other. But thinking back over these we can visualise once more all those who built and destroyed in the Border, who struggled to failure or achievement in the rough but virile life of the past.

In conclusion, may I suggest that few parts of Britain have experienced so little fundamental change as the Border Country. Even the rapid changes of our own time have left largely untouched its basic economy and way of life. With this in mind, we may assert that no part of the country will have a greater appeal to those who feel impelled to escape the evils that seem attendant on modern life. Not only enjoyment but content-ment will be the reward of those who seek the romance of its history, the essential peace of its dales and the unspoiled solitude of the Border hills.

Index

The most important page references are given first. The numerals in **heavy type** denote the page numbers of the illustrations.